COASTAL WRITERS' REFERENCE

COASTAL CAROLINA UNIVERSITY
DEPARTMENT OF ENGLISH

FOUNTAINHEAD
PRESS

Our "green" initiatives include:

Electronic Products

We deliver products in non-paper form whenever possible. This includes pdf downloadables, flash drives, & CDs.

Electronic Samples

We use Xample, a new electronic sampling system. Instructor samples are sent via a personalized web page that links to pdf downloads.

FSC Certified Printers

All of our printers are certified by the Forest Service Council which promotes environmentally and socially responsible management of the world's forests. This program allows consumer groups, individual consumers, and businesses to work together hand-in-hand to promote responsible use of the world's forests as a renewable and sustainable resource.

Recycled Paper

Most of our products are printed on a minimum of 30% post-consumer waste recycled paper.

Support of Green Causes

When we do print, we donate a portion of our revenue to green causes. Listed below are a few of the organizations that have received donations from Fountainhead Press. We welcome your feedback and suggestions for contributions, as we are always searching for worthy initiatives.

Rainforest 2 Reef

Environmental Working Group

Cover design by Doris Bruey

Photo provided by Coastal Carolina Department of English

Book design by Donovan & Gilhooley

Books may be purchased for educational purposes.

For information, please call or write:

1-800-586-0330

Fountainhead Press

2140 E. Southlake Blvd. Ste L #816

Southlake, TX 76092

Web site: www.fountainheadpress.com

E-mail: customerservice@fountainheadpress.com

ISBN: 978-1-68036-049-3

Printed in the United States of America

Contents

Acknowledgements

The *First-Year Composition Guide* has shaped the work of composition courses at Coastal Carolina University since 2009 by providing students with a sense of what to expect as they enter the world of college writing. But that text has provided more than just an introduction to ENGL 101 and 102; it also presents a clear explanation of why working with sources is central to academic writing and provides resources for employing a variety of citation styles. In light of this extended usefulness, the Composition Committee decided to rename the book the *Coastal Writers' Reference* to reflect its suitability for writers across campus.

This newly renamed text is a direct extension of the first three editions of the *First-Year Composition Guide*. As such, we would like to thank those who wrote those editions. We are very grateful that Ellen Arnold, Rebecca Hamill, and Linda Martin began the tradition of the *Guide* by composing a book that informed the work of all instructors and students across our writing program. We also thank Linda Martin and Steve McCartney, who spent long hours revising the *Guide* to create the second edition with Denise Paster in 2011. The *Guide* underwent another substantial revision in 2013 when Catherine Harris, David Kellogg, Denise Paster, Scott Pleasant, Sara Sobota, and Shannon Stewart revised it once again. The *Coastal Writers' Reference* carries on an important collaborative project that anchors the work of our composition classes.

In a stroke of interdisciplinary collaboration, Paul Olsen has graciously allowed us to include *Stare Steps II* in this text. Not only is this image striking, but it also speaks to many of the points we hope to make about writing in this text.

We also want to express appreciation for all students of writing at Coastal Carolina University. While we hope this book is used across campus and in a variety of classes, we are especially committed to the students who are finding their place in this academic setting as they write for our first-year program. The student authors included in this collection—Mikayla Barnwell, Alexander Mosier, Shelby Nicosia, Alessandro Parisi, Alexa Poirier, and Jami Pulley—demonstrate the rich work completed in these classes, and we thank them for generously sharing their texts. Their pieces represent the potential of both the first-year writer and the composition classroom as a whole.

Finally, we thank all instructors of composition at Coastal Carolina University. We feel lucky to work in with a community of teachers who strive to support their students as they explore and embrace literacy practices central to academic work. This is no easy task, and the time, energy, and innovation these instructors bring to their classrooms make this first-year composition program dynamic and successful.

Amanda Grefski   Christian Smith

Denise Paster   Sara Sobota

Scott Pleasant   Shannon Stewart

Practices Central to First-Year Composition 1

We open this chapter with *Stare Steps* II, an image by Paul Olsen (a professor of graphic design here at Coastal Carolina University), because this image suggests the ways in which many writers describe their experiences with successful writing. The image's winding staircase of ever-expanding triangles reminds us that composing is a cyclical process requiring the development of interlocking skills and complex relationships. Although you can find triangular images in the opening pages of many textbooks on writing that point to three important points (such as writer, reader, and topic), those simple three-sided shapes fail to sufficiently convey the complexities we at Coastal associate with writing; they lack the dimensions of stages, strategies, and considerations central to the act of writing.

In our perspective, good writing is always linked to two other important academic skills: careful reading and critical thinking. The First-Year Composition Program at Coastal Carolina University is based on developing connections among these three abilities. So, the three sides of a triangle represent the three "learning outcomes" of the First-Year Composition Program, the three areas of focus in your class: **reading**, **writing**, and **critical thinking**.

The multiple triangles in this photograph (as stairs build upon stairs) also point to the triangular relationships that exist among **writer, reader**, and **subject** – the three elements that affect all writing from Facebook statuses to lab reports to seminar papers. Think about it: Do you write text messages to your parents the same way you do to your friends? Do you use the same tone, the exact vocabulary, or similar styles when writing a note to your roommate versus an email to your professor? We hope not! The purposes that guide your writing and the relationships you establish with your audiences determine what you write and how you write it. You already make these kinds of decisions as you communicate, but in First-Year Composition, you'll learn to make them more intentionally.

Another triangular relationship central to writing is the three-step, recursive process of **prewriting**, **writing**, and **rewriting**. Writing happens in a series of steps that can lead you from confusion through discovery to enlightenment, from the blank screen to a polished essay that will reach out to readers. Far from occurring magically or immediately, writing, for most of us, involves serious effort, like climbing a long and winding staircase. Also like climbing, the effort of writing leads to a big payoff at the end: perhaps a rewarding grade, a nod of understanding, or a smile from your reader.

The First-Year Composition Program

Two composition courses are required under Goal 1A of the Coastal Carolina University (CCU) Core Curriculum:

→ ENGL 101 Composition

→ ENGL 102 Composition and Critical Reading

This requirement means that you must pass these courses with a **C** or better in order to graduate from CCU. The University *Catalog* states that all graduates of CCU will possess knowledge of effective communication and that "[e]ducated persons should have the ability to comprehend, analyze and critically evaluate language, and to express themselves clearly and effectively. Educated persons should be skilled in reading, writing and thinking critically." In sum, all students who earn an adequate grade in Core Goal 1A should be capable readers, writers, and thinkers.

Therefore, both of the composition courses you take are designed to help you develop your skills in understanding and using language – skills you will use throughout your college career and beyond. The English Department separates those abilities into three categories, or student learning outcomes, and each of those categories breaks down into the following skills you should be able to enact by the time you complete the two-course composition sequence.

Student Learning Outcomes

1. **Reading.** To **demonstrate the ability to comprehend and analyze language**, you'll need to show that you can read with understanding and purpose by doing the following:

   ✓ Integrate quotations smoothly and appropriately into your writing.

   ✓ Summarize and paraphrase sources accurately, and acknowledge (cite) your sources honestly.

   ✓ Synthesize multiple written sources, using several sources to support one point or discussing likenesses and differences among several sources.

2. **Writing.** To **demonstrate the ability to express yourself clearly and effectively**, you must fulfill the following expectations for successful writing:

   ✓ Establish a main point, a focus, or an argument (a thesis).

   ✓ Provide supporting reasons or evidence.

   ✓ Organize and structure the project logically.

   ✓ Employ varied sentence structure, effective diction, and an engaging style.

   ✓ Conform to conventional mechanics, spelling, and grammar.

3. **Thinking Critically.** To **demonstrate the ability to comprehend, analyze, and critically evaluate information**, you must use critical thinking in the following ways:

   ✓ Choose appropriate, reliable written sources.

   ✓ Respond to and comment on written sources.

   ✓ Critique written sources.

You might have already practiced some of these skills in high school, but your First-Year Composition instructors will expect you to show progress in sharpening them. Instructors will also use the above learning outcomes to structure their classes, to craft writing assignments, and to establish grading criteria. Though individual teachers draw on a variety of approaches while designing and teaching composition classes, they all work to support you as you reach for these goals.

REMEMBER: You must pass ENGL 101 and 102 with a **C** or better in order to satisfy this Core requirement.

The First-Year Composition Program's Goals

Since all First-Year Composition courses share the same goals and outcomes, students in all courses can expect to encounter a variety of writing projects, read and discuss samples of effective writing, and practice skills such as summary, synthesis, analysis, argument, and critique. Specific strategies, class activities, and writing assignments will vary by course and section, but all First-Year Composition courses will focus on academic writing—the kind of writing expected in most college classrooms.

Working with texts by responding to the words and ideas of others through quoting, paraphrasing, and summarizing is central to academic writing. By stressing these skills, First-Year Composition classes highlight the importance of joining the larger community of college writers. In responding to texts, students add to conversations already in progress. That is, it is not enough to write about your ideas on a given topic; instead, you should contribute to a larger conversation about an issue through your writing. In order to add to such conversations in meaningful ways, you need to situate your responses in light of what others have said before. So, while your English classes in high school might have asked you to follow certain writing conventions (such as using the five paragraph essay format and quoting correctly), First-Year Composition courses ask that you use your writing to develop your thinking about a particular topic, concern, or question while you consider what others have written before you. These courses ask that you enter the larger, ongoing conversations that are carried on through academic texts.

Scholars and professionals write to and for one another, creating communities that grapple with issues central to particular disciplines and professions. Because these communities are constructed by ongoing conversations in journals, in books, and at conferences, the research you do for your composition classes allows you to understand and access communities that speak to your professional and scholarly goals. For example, if you are committed to issues of sustainability, you will want to gain a sense of where others publish their stands on current environmental issues. If you hope to enter the field of hospitality, you will need to gain a sense of where the latest resort trends are published. To join these kinds of conversations, you will respond to them in the margins of actual texts, in written responses, during class, on your class website, and in more developed essays. Through these responses, you enter larger academic discourse communities, which are, in many ways, constructed by written interactions.

You must also consider the ways in which you enter and position yourself within such contexts. As a writer working to enter an ongoing conversation, you will need to consider how you refer to other writers and their work and how to weave their thinking, ideas, and words into your own texts. Properly introducing, citing, and documenting quotations and paraphrases will show that you are aware of the turns others have taken in text-based conversations as you build on previously published views, ideas, and conclusions.

This consideration and incorporation of outside sources entails paying attention to intellectual integrity. To maintain academic and professional standards, you'll want to use the work of other writers in ways that fairly present their views, credit their perspectives, and document how you are drawing on their ideas and words. Attending to such practices will not only help you avoid plagiarism (see the Plagiarism section in chapter two for a more complete definition), but will also show that you value the intellectual work of others.

While your First-Year Composition courses will not (and cannot) teach you how to write for every situation, they will call your attention to the importance of understanding the situations you enter as a writer whenever you take on a new task. By focusing on the writing process and the significance of reflection, these classes strive to make you a conscientious writer who is aware of the importance of context. These classes teach strategies that are central to academic writing, strategies you will build upon as you write for other classes and professional settings.

First-Year Composition Courses

In **ENGL 101**, **Composition**, students focus on the writing process, paying special attention to prewriting, writing, and revising strategies. The course also introduces elements of academic writing as well as the research process. This class prompts students to hone their critical reading and writing skills as they consider the rhetorical situations that shape all writing tasks. As a hybrid course, ENGL 101 includes a parallel online component, Coastal Composition Commons, which provides digitally delivered content reinforcing a common set of student learning outcomes.

English 101 focuses on the writing process—by stressing the importance of pre-writing, writing, and rewriting—and examines the connections among writer, reader, and subject. As you work through ENGL 101, you will attend to the inter-sections of critical reading, thinking, and writing. Remember the triangle formed by the stairs depicted on the first page of this chapter? That image points to the importance of all of these triangular aspects of composition.

This course also focuses on essay writing, which may take the form of narratives, descriptions, profiles, reviews, and research papers. As a student of Composition, you will be presented with a variety of reading and writing scenarios and will have to think about your audience and purpose as you compose rhetorically effective texts. No matter what genre you work in, you will be moving into the world of academic writing as you use your writing to respond to both the thinking and words of others—moves central to most intellectual work.

So, in addition to focusing on the writing process and essay writing, ENGL 101 also concentrates on research strategies. As you move through this class, you will bring both primary and secondary sources into your writing as you gather, analyze, and critique information. Using outside sources in these ways will enable you to come to your own conclusions as you consider others' perspectives regarding a spectrum of issues, questions, and topics.

In **ENGL 102**, **Composition and Critical Reading**, students read and respond to a variety of texts written across disciplinary lines. As they interpret and evaluate these texts by composing functional, rhetorical, and critical analyses, students extend their understanding of the writing process, consider the importance of context, and refine their approaches to research. This hybrid course includes a parallel online component, Coastal Composition Commons, which builds upon the content taught in ENGL 101 and incorporates digital material that stresses an ongoing set of common student learning outcomes.

To prepare you further for the kinds of reading and writing you will be asked to complete across and beyond campus, ENGL 102 introduces readings from a variety of disciplines and provides you with approaches for actively analyzing a range of genres. In this class, which builds upon the skills and strategies introduced in ENGL 101, you can expect to write rhetorical analyses, visual analyses, critiques, arguments, and informative and evaluative syntheses. In short, much of the writing you do for Composition and Critical Reading will be in response to other texts, which will derive from an array of topical fields.

In addition to exposing you to readings that cross disciplinary boundaries, ENGL 102 also asks that you compose careful and close analyses of these pieces by considering the ways they are situated by contexts -- historical, political, and social. So, this class asks you to display an understanding of how texts function in particular settings for particular purposes, and it invites you to question the rhetorical nature of texts. Such experiences will prepare you to enact the kinds of reading and analysis you will be expected to employ in upper level courses.

Coastal Composition Commons

Coastal Composition Commons (ccc.coastal.edu) is a digital badge initiative that stresses the student learning outcomes central to ENGL 101 and 102. Each digital badge provides instruction on a skill important to your development as a writer and is designed to help you complete the writing required in your first-year writing course. The completion of these digital badges is central to your success in First-Year Composition and supports your development as a writer in more general terms. Each badge has been designed with the course goals in mind, and they are meant to make the literate activities that anchor these classes (such as summarizing, paraphrasing, and shaping a thesis) even more visible.

Your instructor will assign these badges throughout the semester and will provide you with a firm due date for each badge. Badge submissions will be approved or denied by your instructor.

Joining the Community of College Writers

As a first-year college writer, you are not only entering Coastal Carolina University and learning the landscape, expectations, and habits associated with this academic setting, but you are also figuring out what it means, in larger terms, to join an academic community—a community that values learning, inquiry, discovery, collaboration, and the sharing of ideas. Thinking of yourself as a student entering an academic community can help you see how your First-Year Composition classes work to enhance your college experience.

By this point, you have a general idea of what you can expect from ENGL 101 and 102. You are probably most concerned, however, with what it takes to be successful in your composition class. Turning to the notion of community can help you figure out what it takes to succeed in most courses, including those you take across campus.

Community is a broad concept. If asked to think about communities you belong to, you could probably list many off the top of your head, such as your family, various groups of friends, church groups, sports teams, and social organizations. To make this term—*community*—a bit more specific, we are going to refer to *discourse communities*. Discourse communities are made up of people who share ways of communicating and acting, as well as ideas, understandings, and expectations.

As speakers and writers, you belong to a variety of discourse communities because you know how to use language and act in ways that best suit particular groups and settings. How you use language with your family at the dinner table is probably different from how you speak to your teammates in the locker room. These shifts in *discourse*—in how you use language: the words you draw on, the tone you establish, the topics you introduce, and the ways in which you engage your listeners—help you position yourself as an insider to particular communities.

As you join the academic discourse community of First-Year Composition, you should build on the understandings about effective language use that you bring to the classroom as you take on the ways of thinking, reading, writing, and participating that will position you as an "insider" to this setting. When you join any new group, you need to figure out how to use language in that setting. You need to figure out how to say, ask, and do things in ways that work for that context. Your composition class is no exception. To make this process easier, every class has policies that are clarified explicitly on a syllabus; the policies for First-Year Composition courses here at Coastal Carolina University are explained in the next chapter. Knowing the course policies and abiding by them are the first steps you can take toward becoming an "insider" to your class.

To be an "insider," you must understand and enact the practices that are central to your First-Year Composition class and outlined in class documents such as this book, your syllabus, and the class textbook. These documents clarify the general things you can do to adopt "insider" ways, but the process of becoming an "insider" doesn't end once you have read, understood, and abided by the policies associated with any given setting. Noticing and tending to what is valued in particular settings, but not explained in explicit ways, will help you fully understand what it takes to become a full insider. So, this process of acculturation, as you become a productive "insider" to your composition class, involves taking on a set of productive practices (which are described below). It also requires that you understand the valued ways of writing, reading, and sharing central to your particular class.

Becoming a Productive Insider to First-Year Composition

Participate Actively in Class. When you get to your First-Year Composition class, be ready to be active. This might mean taking notes, answering questions, asking questions, working in groups, contributing to discussions, listening carefully to what others are saying, returning to texts to revisit a reaction you had when reading, or making new notations in the margins of your book. In sum, come to class ready to share your ideas, reactions, and experiences.

While active participation is valued in most academic discourse communities, it is especially important in composition classes. Being an active participant means you should come to class on time, complete all assigned activities, and be ready to comment on the course materials. So, while avoiding absences is important, it is not enough just to be in class. You need to be prepared to contribute actively to class in order to be successful in this discourse community.

Being active in class also means being focused, and digital distractions will prevent you from being attentive. Texting, checking your email, or engaging in any other activities (completing an assignment for another class, for instance) that take your attention away from your class, your teacher, and your classmates, will mark you as an "outsider," a student who is not invested in this classroom community. You don't want this to happen.

As an active participant, you should grapple with course materials in serious ways by approaching them as a careful and questioning reader, but you should also be mindful of how you interact with your instructor and your classmates. In academic settings, an environment of respectful engagement, active collaboration, and systematic inquiry is the ideal; creating such a context entails cultivating productive relationships that establish you and your classmates as colleagues who respect one another and acknowledge the guidance and expertise of your instructor.

To contribute to your class in productive ways, you need to understand the qualities of an active student. Here is a guide that will help you understand the importance of active learning and how you can take responsibility for your academic success.

Remember that just as you are figuring out what it takes to be an insider to your section of composition, your instructor is also assessing your performance as a student. How you act during class matters and is central to how your instructor and classmates understand you. Use this rubric to identify your own areas of strength and weakness as you work to become an active contributor to your class.

(Rubric adapted from http://culter.colorado.edu/~kittel/ParticptnCriteria.pdf)

The "A" Student

→ initiates and maintains interaction with students and instructor from the beginning of class

→ shows leadership in group activities

→ attempts to draw connections between course material

→ is willing to help other students understand the material

→ is always prepared for class

The "B" Student

→ shows willingness to participate

→ cooperates fully in discussions and group activities although may not necessarily be the leader

→ answers questions readily when called upon

→ elaborates somewhat on answers

→ is prepared for class most days

The "C" Student

→ participates more passively than actively

→ is off topic or distracting, especially in small group activities

→ does not elaborate on answers or statements

→ is frequently unprepared

The "D" Student

→ participates grudgingly

→ is unresponsive or overly controlling in discussions and small group activities

→ generally does not cooperate in group activities

→ is usually unprepared for class

The "F" Student

→ is unable to answer when called upon in class

→ is disruptive and prevents others from learning

→ rarely participates in class activities

→ is disrespectful of other students and the instructor

→ has a negative attitude, refuses to answer questions, and constantly introduces unwarranted criticism of other students and/or the instructor

→ is obviously unprepared

Bring Your Textbooks. When you complete assigned readings, take notes and pose questions you are left with in the margins. This kind of active reading will keep you alert as you look for points to comment on or question, and it will prepare you to discuss and write about the texts you read.

While this kind of active reading is useful on its own, having your books in class will provide you with a "map" of your responses and reactions to a text as you can skim your notes to see what points were especially striking to you. Simply buying the required texts will not guarantee academic success; using these texts actively and spending a lot of time with them, both in and out of class, is a step toward becoming an insider to this academic community.

Determine What Your Instructor Wants. One of the questions students frequently ask is, "How much work will I need to do to get a decent grade in this class?" Instructors have individual ideas about what is needed to create a successful semester. Some instructors hope their students fully explore their writing processes and take full advantage of the revision process. Other instructors may tailor a course around a particular theme such as environmental concerns, politics, or social issues in hopes that their students develop complex understandings regarding these matters. Still other instructors are looking for students to become experts in creating an MLA formatted document. As a learner, you will need to identify the goals central to your section of composition and find ways to best achieve them.

Keep in mind, though, that while instructors have individual goals for their courses, they all expect students to be responsible members of their classes who do their best in each meeting and on each task. Paying attention to what seems important in your class—to what reading, writing, and participatory practices seem expected of students—is the first step in figuring out what it takes to "make it." This is true of every new situation (class, job, social scene) you enter.

Develop a Relationship with Your Instructor. Establishing a strong rapport with your composition instructor will help you figure out what is valued in this academic setting. Coastal Carolina University instructors keep regular office hours every week throughout the semester. Instructors are generally delighted to have students come by their offices. Once the semester is fully underway, however, it is advisable to email your instructor to set up an appointment. Utilizing your professor's office hours can be extremely useful, as it allows time to discuss individual issues in ways that are just not possible during class meetings.

In addition to office hours, you can also use email to support a productive working relationship with your professors. While you will not want to inundate them with emails, sending your professors a message before unavoidably missing a class can go a long way. When emailing your instructors, you will not use the same writing style you use when emailing a close friend or family member. Faculty members appreciate receiving emails that are addressed formally and explicitly to them that include your full name, the course and section you are enrolled in, and a carefully written explanation of your comment, concern, or question.

You will also gain much from reading comments and feedback from your instructor carefully. When you receive any kind of feedback, read it along with your original text and make notations next to the comments (maybe noting what you will keep in mind as you write your next paper) and be sure to ask your instructor any questions you might have about this feedback. These comments are, in many ways, a conversation between you and your instructor; fully understanding the logic and reasoning behind them can only help you become a stronger writer.

Develop Relationships with your Classmates. It is clearly important to develop a productive and professional relationship with your instructor. As a student in a First-Year Composition course, though, you also need to establish a productive rapport with your classmates. By listening to their comments intently and thinking carefully about their perspectives, you will come to richer understandings of your own work and about writing in general. Collaborative work is critically important in First-Year Composition courses, as it provides opportunities to think through a text, issue, or question with others. When you get into groups to complete work, this is no time to use the restroom or check your email. This is time to do the important work of collaborative thinking, a skill required in most academic and professional settings.

In many classes, you will work through peer review activities. In the past, you might have mainly worked to "correct" your classmates' writing by locating and marking errors during peer review sessions. As you work to review your classmates' writing in ENGL 101 and 102, you should focus on larger, more global issues as you think through your classmates' texts. Be sure to consider the arguments they make as well as the structure of their writing. Question how they move between generalizations and specific examples in their writing to make and develop points. Assess the tone and style they establish in their writing in light of their purposes and audience. Taking such approaches will help you develop your understandings of strong and persuasive writing, and it will also help you provide your classmates with comments that will help them rethink the texts they are revising. Move beyond comments like, "This looks good. Just work on your grammar." Instead, provide feedback that offers suggestions for revising and reworking a text.

Learn the Implicit Rules. To reiterate, becoming an insider to any discourse community, whether that community is made up of a new group of friends or new work colleagues, involves figuring out what goes unsaid. In most situations, no one pulls you aside and says, "Listen, in this group, we can joke about Matt's taste in music, but Jimmy's car is off limits." These are the kinds of things you learn by trial and error and, more productively, through careful observation. As we've noted throughout this chapter, the same goes for academic discourse communities. So, while attending to official course materials is undeniably important in figuring out what is valued, observing how your particular class functions while noting the implicit rules regarding what it takes to be an insider is also integral. As a savvy writer, reader, and thinker, you should always be analyzing the contexts you work within so you can make fully informed decisions about your participation.

Policies Central to First-Year Composition 2

While your instructor and syllabus will provide you with much information regarding what is required in your section of ENGL 101 or 102, this chapter presents an overview of what is expected across all sections.

All First-Year Composition courses adhere to the general University regulations as explained in the CCU *Catalog*. Some policies are explained here to provide a clear idea of what it takes to succeed in these courses. If you are looking for a more detailed discussion of academic regulations at Coastal Carolina University, go to http://www.coastal.edu/academics/catalog/.

Attendance. Attendance is essential to your success in First-Year Composition. An instructor may impose a penalty, including assigning the grade of **F**, for unexcused absences in excess of 25% of the regularly scheduled class meetings.

The CCU *Catalog* excuses absences for **documented** cases of

1. Incapacitating illness

2. Official representation of the University

3. Death of a close relative

4. Religious holidays

An instructor may require a more stringent class attendance policy. Use the following lines to record your instructor's attendance policy:

_____

_____

_____

MAKEUP WORK. As stated in the CCU *Catalog*, absences, excused or not, do not absolve you from the responsibility of completing all assigned work promptly.

Students who miss assignments, announced quizzes, or other coursework obligations due to **excused** absences (as defined above) will be allowed to make up the work in a manner deemed appropriate by their instructor. If you are absent for an excused reason, it is your responsibility to contact your instructor as soon as possible by phone or e-mail to make up the work that you missed at your instructor's convenience.

Your instructor is not obligated to allow you to make up work missed due to an unexcused absence. In fact, most instructors will not allow make-up work for unexcused absences. However, if you know beforehand that you will be unavoidably absent on a day when a test is scheduled or a paper is due, see your instructor ahead of time to see if you can arrange a make-up date.

Use the following lines to record your instructor's policy on makeup work or late work:

_____

_____

_____

Final Exam. A final exam is required in all First-Year Composition classes. As stated in the CCU *Catalog*, a student who is absent from the final examination will be given the grade **F** in the course if an excuse acceptable to the instructor has not been offered. Final exams are typically held during the Block I exam period (on the Monday of exam week, from 8:30–10:30). Use the following space to record the time, date, and location of the final exam for your class:

_____

_____

_____

Statement on Disabilities and Accommodations. Students who identify themselves as having disabilities are referred to the Office of Disability Services. This office is responsible for ensuring that reasonable accommodations are provided for students with documented learning, physical, and psychological disabilities. If you have a documented disability, please contact the Office of Disability Services at 843-349-2341. This office will then coordinate efforts with you and your instructor to be sure that you are accommodated.

Plagiarism. It is the English department's policy that plagiarism, even a first offense, will earn a failing grade for academic dishonesty (**FX**) in the course. Plagiarism is defined as "presenting as one's own the work or the opinions of someone else." Most students define plagiarism as "copying material of some sort, either word for word or sense for sense." Although that definition is accurate, the criterion is not merely copying exact words; ideas, conclusions, and ways of organizing material can also be plagiarized.

Specifically, one is guilty of plagiarism when:

1. The words, sentences, ideas, conclusions, examples, and/or organization of an assignment are borrowed from a source (a book, an article, another student's paper, etc.) without acknowledging the source.

2. A student submits another's work in lieu of his/her own assignment.

3. A student allows another person to revise, correct, or in any way rewrite his/her assignment without having the prior approval of the instructor.

4. A student submits written assignments received from commercial firms, "paper mill" websites, fraternity or sorority files, or any other outside source.

5. A student allows another person to take all or part of his/her course.

6. A student submits an assignment (a paper, a library assignment, a revision, etc.) done together with another student without having approval from the instructor.

A student who knowingly aids another student in plagiarizing an assignment as defined in 1–6 above will also earn a failing grade (**FX**) in the course.

As explained in the *Catalog*, **FX** is assigned for courses where failure occurs as a result of academic dishonesty. The **FX** grade is treated as an **F** in the grade point average computation. Courses that receive an **FX** grade are not eligible to be repeated under the University's "Repeat Forgiveness" option, and instead may only be repeated via the "Standard Repeat" option. When assigned, the **FX** grade will become a part of the student's internal academic record and will appear on unofficial transcripts and within the student information system. The **FX** grade will appear as an **F** on the student's official transcript.

For more information about the "Code of Student Conduct and Academic Responsibility," see the CCU *Student Handbook*. To signify that you have read and understood the plagiarism policy for First-Year Composition, your instructor will ask you to sign and turn in the Plagiarism Statement sheet that follows.

ENGL 101
Tear-out Plagiarism Statement for First-Year Composition

Sign the following Plagiarism statement, tear it out, and turn it in to your instructor.

It is the English department's policy that plagiarism, even a first offense, will earn a failing grade (**FX**) for the course. Plagiarism is defined as "presenting as one's own the work or the opinions of someone else." Most students define plagiarism as "copying material of some sort, either word for word or sense for sense." Although that definition is accurate, the criterion is not merely copying wording; ideas, conclusions, and ways of organizing material can also be plagiarized.

Specifically, one is guilty of plagiarism when:

1. The words, sentences, ideas, conclusions, examples, and/or organization of an assignment are borrowed from a source (a book, an article, another student's paper, etc.) without acknowledging the source.

2. A student submits another's work in lieu of his/her own assignment.

3. A student allows another person to revise, correct, or in any way rewrite his/her assignment without having the prior approval of the instructor.

4. A student submits written assignments received from commercial firms, fraternity or sorority files, or any other outside source.

5. A student allows another person to take all or part of his/her course.

6. A student submits an assignment (a paper, a library assignment, a revision, etc.) done together with another student without having approval from the instructor.

A student who knowingly aids another student in plagiarizing an assignment as defined in 1–6 above will also earn a failing grade (**FX**) in the course.

By signing below, I certify that I have read and understood the above plagiarism policy for first-year composition.

_____   _____

(Student signature)   (Date)

_____

(Print name)

_____   _____

(Instructor's name)   (Course/Section)

Tear-Out Quiz:
First-Year Composition Syllabus and Course Policies

Use the *Coastal Writers' Reference*, your class syllabus, and your notes to answer the following questions.

1. When are your instructor's office hours? Where can you meet with your instructor during these times?

2. What is your instructor's attendance policy?

3. What is your instructor's policy on accepting late work?

4. Which of the following are examples of plagiarism?

   A. emailing your paper to your mom for editing

   B. borrowing an idea from Wikipedia, expressing it in your own words but not citing your source

   C. writing a paper with a friend without prior permission from your instructor

   D. using exact words from a source without quotation marks or citation

   E. all of the above

5. What is the penalty for plagiarism in First-Year Composition?

   A. penalty depends on the instructor

   B. failing grade on the assignment

   C. no grade on the assignment with a chance to rewrite

   D. F in the class with a chance for grade forgiveness

   E. FX in the class (no grade forgiveness)

6. Which of the following is **not** considered an excused absence?

   A. documented traffic court appearance

   B. documented incapacitating illness

   C. documented official representation of the University

   D. documented death of a close relative

   E. religious holiday

7. When is the final exam for your First-Year Composition class?

8. What grade must you earn in ENGL 101 and 102 in order to satisfy Core requirements?

9. What are the three categories of Student Learning Outcomes for First-Year Composition courses?

   A. writer, reader, subject matter

   B. prewriting, writing, rewriting

   C. reading, writing, thinking critically

10. Instructor's choice

Resources for Writers at Coastal Carolina University

The Writing Center

Kearns Building Room 203
www.coastal.edu/writingcenter
843-349-2937

The Writing Center—located in Kearns 203—serves all students on the CCU campus but first-year writing students are especially encouraged to make use of its services. Students who come to the Writing Center participate in a one-on-one consultation with a member of the Writing Center staff. Most of our staff members are undergraduate students who have excelled in their writing courses at Coastal, but you might see a graduate student or the Coordinator of the Center when you come for a writing consultation.

These consultations are typically thirty minutes in length, but may be somewhat shorter or longer. During the session, you and a tutor can work on any aspect of the paper, from the beginning stages when you are developing your ideas to the final stages when you are polishing your writing and making sure your paper is formatted correctly.

Some high schools have writing centers, but most do not, so many first-year students have not had any experience with the kind of assistance that a writing center can provide. It is important to point out that visiting the Writing Center is not a sign that you are a poor writer. All good writers review their work with others. In fact, research has shown that strong writers get just as much out of a writing center tutorial as weaker writers. If you struggle with writing, the Writing Center can certainly help you, but we want to see stronger writers, too. If you're a strong enough writer, you might even want to work in the Writing Center one day!

When you visit the Writing Center, the tutor will probably begin by asking you what you would like to work on in the session and what you are trying to accomplish in your paper. Then, you and your tutor will usually read some of the paper together (or all of it if it is a short paper). You will spend the majority of your thirty-minute session discussing ideas for improving the paper. The focus in each session is different because each student and each writing assignment are unique, but you can expect to receive individual assistance that helps you improve specific aspects of the paper, perhaps the thesis statement or the introductory or concluding paragraph—whatever you and the tutor decide to work on.

After each session, the tutor writes a detailed report that is sent to your teacher by e-mail. In the report, the tutor identifies the assignment the two of you worked on, the features in the paper that you focused on, and the plan for improvement that you and the tutor discussed. Your teachers will be pleased to see that you have visited the Writing Center. However, if you would rather for some reason that the report not be sent to your teacher, simply tell the tutor that you don't want the report to be sent.

We recommend that you make an appointment when you want to visit the Writing Center because we are sometimes quite busy. If you make an appointment, you will be guaranteed a thirty-minute time slot. Just call the Center at (843) 349-2937 to make an appointment or drop by Kearns 203 to set up an appointment in person. Walk-in students are welcome, too, but are not always guaranteed to be seen right away. If all tutors are busy when you try to walk in, you may be asked to make an appointment for later that day or for another day.

If you have any questions about the Writing Center, please feel free to write an e-mail to writingcenter@coastal.edu or call the Writing Center Coordinator, Scott Pleasant, at (843) 349-4154. We hope to see you at the Writing Center often during your first year and beyond!

Kimbel Library and Bryan Information Commons

www.coastal.edu/library
843-349-2400

Kimbel Library exists to meet the diverse research needs of the campus community. You can take advantage of many of the library's resources online or visit in person for face-to-face research help.

Student Computing Services

Kimbel Library Room 204
www.coastal.edu/scs
843-349-2908

Student Computing Services (SCS) assists students with technical issues and questions. If you are working on a technology related project, SCS will also help you find the appropriate resources, use these technologies, and answer questions you might have.

Satellite Computer Labs

The CAI Lab
Prince 204
843-349-2908

The Edwards Computer Lab
Edwards 171
843-349-2377

The Wall Computer Lab
Wall 108
843-349-2351

The Science Computer Lab
Science 122
843-349-2571

Venues for Sharing Your Writing at Coastal Carolina University

The Paul Rice Poetry Broadside Series is a competition open to currently enrolled Coastal Carolina University students. Each year, student submissions in poetry are judged by an independent panel.

Tempo Magazine is CCU's features magazine that comes out each semester. *Tempo* looks for writers with a strong voice who want to have an impact on the student body. Staff members write articles as they choose, depending on which topics they are passionate about. *Tempo* prides itself on covering issues that don't always make their way into mainstream college media.

Archarios is published annually and is unveiled in the spring. The magazine publishes student poetry, short stories, photography and artwork collected and judged twice during the academic school year.

The Weekly Chant is CCU's weekly newspaper that is produced by students. Meetings are held weekly and open to all students who are interested in writing, editing, designing layouts, drawing cartoons and taking pictures. Students do not need to be English majors to be involved; all are welcomed and encouraged to participate in producing CCU's newspaper.

Bridges is a multi-disciplinary, online scholarly journal produced annually. This journal seeks to provide a forum for exploring issues and ideas that go beyond boundaries devoted to specific disciplines/majors. *Bridges* is dedicated to creative and integrative knowledge and thought.

The Best Essay Contest celebrates the strongest writing composed in First-Year Composition classes. Papers are nominated by instructors, reviewed by a panel of faculty readers, and then judged by the Officers of Sigma Tau Delta (the English Honor Society). The top essays are then recognized during the Spring Sigma Tau Delta Induction Ceremony.

We have included some winning essays from past contests in chapter seven of this book. Though they are not perfect, these essays serve as examples of excellent first-year writing as they all share common characteristics:

→ They show originality in approach to the topic and development.

→ They use a distinctive, appropriate voice that conveys a sophisticated or personal style.

→ They present a clear thesis.

→ They are effectively organized.

→ They are grammatically and mechanically clean (though not necessarily perfect).

→ They use diction appropriate to audience and purpose.

→ If applicable, they conform to MLA/APA manuscript conventions, including MLA/APA documentation.

→ If applicable, they draw upon varied and appropriate sources and effectively integrate outside source material.

If you have an essay that you have written for a First-Year Composition course that you are particularly proud of, we invite you to ask your instructor to submit it to the contest. Fill out the form on the next page, attach it to a copy of your essay, and pass those documents along to your instructor to submit to the Coordinator of Composition. Then email a digital version of your essay along with a reflection on the process of writing your essay or on advice you have for other student writers (as a .doc, .docx, or PDF) directly to Denise Paster, the current Coordinator of Composition, at dpaster@coastal.edu. Who knows? You may see your work published in the next edition of the *Coastal Writers' Reference*.

Essay Submission Cover Sheet

First-Year Writing Award

Coastal Carolina University

Name: _____

Phone: _____

Email:_____

Mailing address (permanent): _____

_____

Essay title: _____

Course: _____

Instructor's name: _____

Please read and sign the statement below:

I hereby submit my essay for consideration for the Coastal Carolina University English Department's First-Year Writing Award. I give permission for my work to be published for use in future English courses.

_____   _____

(Student Signature)   (Date)

Student:

1. Complete this sheet.

2. Print your essay.

3. Staple this sheet to the front of your essay.

4. On a separate document, comment on the process of writing your essay or on advice you have for other student writers. What did you learn from writing this essay? What seems important about how you wrote this piece? What should other first-year writers keep in mind when composing? Staple this to your essay.

5. Submit these texts (this form, your reflection, and your essay) to your instructor.

6. Email a copy of your essay as an attachment to Denise Paster at dpaster@ coastal.edu. In the subject line of this email please write "First-Year Writing Award" and include your reflection. Please attach your work using one of the following formats: .doc, .docx, or PDF.

Instructor: Give the essay and cover sheet to the Coordinator of Composition by the end of the semester.

Sample Grading Rubric

To write your best, you need to understand the qualities of good writing. This checklist is meant to provide some understanding of what your instructor will be looking for in your writing and your development as a writer.

An "A" Paper

→ opens clearly and has a tight focus (thesis)

→ makes interesting, specific observations

→ pursues points with examples and details; explains clearly, creatively and completely

→ is easy to read and understand because wording is precise and sentences well structured

→ has only one or two very minor grammatical errors (i.e. a missing comma)

→ has a conclusion that effectively drives home the point the writer is making

→ leaves readers feeling they have learned something significant

→ uses scholarly sources and cites them correctly

A "B" Paper

→ opens clearly and has a tight focus

→ makes some good observations

→ tries to pursue points, but may be short on examples or explanation in places

→ is clearly written and easy to follow, but the wording is not always on target and some sentences are a bit too wordy

→ has only a few minor grammatical errors

→ may have a conclusion that merely repeats information without driving home the main point

→ makes readers feel convinced but not enlightened

→ uses some scholarly sources and cites them correctly for the most part

A "C" Paper*

→ opens clearly, but does not provide a narrow enough focus

→ makes one or two specific observations, but remains vague or general

→ has some examples and detail, but descriptions and explanations fall short

→ has sentences that are not always clear, the wording is not precise, and sentences are cluttered with unnecessary phrases

→ has some major grammatical errors that cause confusion, such as subject-verb disagreement, misspellings, comma splices, and fragments

→ may have a conclusion that merely repeats information without making a point

→ leaves readers unconvinced

→ rarely uses scholarly sources and does not follow conventions when citing sources

A "D" Paper

→ may open by making a clear point, but doesn't stick to it

→ may make some specific observations, but this paper is mostly made up of vague notions, redundant statements, or emotional responses

→ provides few examples and details, and these are not always relevant to the point

→ has sentences that are cluttered with unnecessary words and lacking in clarity

→ has major grammatical errors

→ may have a redundant conclusion

→ leaves readers unconvinced and confused

→ perhaps uses one scholarly source and does not correctly cite sources

An "F" paper

→ is very seriously flawed or does not follow assignment guidelines

→ has an opening that is unclear; it's hard to see what point the writer is making

→ provides vague responses and lacks specific examples

→ provides almost no textual detail or examples

→ has cluttered, unclear sentences that are hard to read

→ has a lot of grammatical errors

→ may have a redundant conclusion

→ is difficult to read and understand

→ may be mainly a personal anecdote that is only tangentially related to the assignment

→ does not use or cite scholarly sources

* Most first-year students write C papers.

Citation Practices

Citation, or documentation, is the practice of writing so that readers can find the sources you use. Citation is a fundamental good habit of all academic writing. *Everybody* in academic life cites—faculty as well as students. Because you will cite the work of other writers throughout your time at Coastal and beyond, the citation skills you develop in ENGL 101 and 102 are crucial to your overall academic success.

Why is citation so central to academic writing? The reasons are many. When you cite:

- You back up your claims. Much academic writing is argumentative: that is, it makes claims that are open to dispute. We make claims based on both reason and evidence, and lots of our evidence comes from what we read. (Other types of evidence include primary research such as observation and controlled experiment.) Citation allows readers to consult the same sources that we have used.

- You invoke powerful friends. When you cite, you create an implicit alliance with those writers and thinkers who are sympathetic to your point of view. You probably have heard a speech where someone has quoted Dr. Martin Luther King, Jr. or Mother Teresa. We cite such sources not merely because they make good points but because readers respect the views of these public figures. By citing them, you create alliances with people that your readers already trust.

- You acknowledge the help you received. Sometimes student writers think their work will be diminished if some of the ideas came from other sources. But academic writing is never wholly original. Academic writers know that research never occurs in a vacuum, and citation can be considered a form of good courtesy or manners.

- You demonstrate professionalism. Citation has become so ingrained in academic life that writing without citation, in most cases, is considered unprofessional. Citation is a mark of a thoughtful, mature, careful, and polished writer. By the same logic, lack of citation makes your writing look thoughtless, immature, careless, and rough.

- You protect yourself. By citing responsibly, you insulate yourself from charges of plagiarism, and you show who is responsible for the claims and information you provide. For many students, this is the main reason for citing. But citation offers a further protection. If you cite carefully, you can ensure that errors made by your *source* will not be attributed to *you*.

For these and many other reasons, you should never ask your instructor, "Do I have to cite my sources?" Unless explicitly told otherwise, assume citation is required.

Types of Citation

It would be nice if there were just one "citation style" or way of citing. That way you could use a single style for everything you write. In academic life, however, citations styles vary from field to field, and even within a field. There are literally hundreds of different styles. Many professional organizations and journals have their own style; after you graduate, you may even work for a corporation that uses a company-specific style guide.

Fortunately, almost all citation styles fall into a few basic categories. The most basic division is between two citation systems: **parenthetical** and **numbered**. A parenthetical system uses parenthetical marks *within* the main text that point to items in reference list at the *end* of the main text. A numbered system uses footnotes or endnotes with a number in the text guiding the reader to the list of notes.

Parenthetical and numbered systems can be further divided into citation types.

- Parenthetical styles are either **Author-Page** or **Author-Date**, depending on whether the parenthesis lists the page number or the year of publication along with the author's last name. In both style types, the reference list at the end of the paper is organized alphabetically by author. Author-Date style types, however, list multiple items by the same author according to year of publication rather than title.

- Numbered styles are either **Note-Bib** or **Numbered List**. The Note-Bib style type uses footnotes or endnotes that refer to a master list of sources consulted (the bibliography). A Numbered List style type simply lists the citations, usually in the order in which they are cited. Note-Bib styles have the advantage that notes can contain additional text other than the reference itself—for example, commentary or qualification. Numbered List styles have the advantage that numbers can be used repeatedly: if you refer to the same source twice, you simply use the same number.

Finally, within each of these four types are different *styles*. The most common Author-Page style is the Modern Language Association (MLA) style. The most common Author-Date style is the American Psychological Association (APA) style. The most common Note-Bib system is based on the Chicago Manual of Style (CMS). **Figure 1** shows how these categories relate to each other, with the boxes on the right listing just a few specific style examples. Note that the Chicago style has both a Notes-Bib and an Author-Date form. To help you with Chicago format, we have included a separate chapter on the CMS system. This chapter illustrates the Notes-Bib form, but it is possible that a teacher will ask you to write in the Author-Date form. So if a professor asks you to use Chicago style, make sure you know which version is required!

You may encounter new styles throughout your academic and professional life.

As a writer, you should become comfortable with whatever system is used most commonly in your field. But don't try to memorize it: instead, get a good book that deals with your citation system at length, and keep it close to hand.

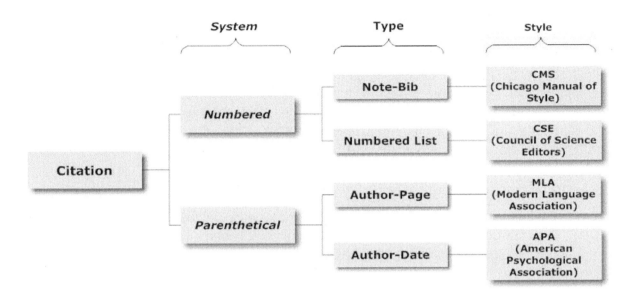

Figure 1: Citation styles and their categories. The two style systems (numbered and parenthetical) break into four basic types and then many individual styles. For purposes of illustration, only one major style is named for each type.

Principles of Citation

Academic citation systems are designed to help readers find sources clearly and efficiently. Within limits, then, all citation systems tend to operate according to two basic principles.

Principle 1: Precision. Whatever you include in the body of a text—a note number, parenthetical reference, or something else—should take you precisely to the citation at the end of the text or the bottom of the page and to no other citation. The citation in turn should take you precisely to the source you consulted and to no other source.

Principle 2: Concision. Whatever you include in the body of a text should include the *minimal* amount of information needed to satisfy the rule of precision. The citation in turn should include *only* what is necessary to locate the precise source.

Let's consider an example. You are probably familiar with the MLA style, since it was most likely used in your high school English classes. In MLA style, you cite by putting the author's last name in a parentheses, along with the page number(s), in the text. Suppose you are writing a paper using MLA style and want to quote a sentence by the linguist Steven Pinker. The sentence, which appears on page 371 of his book *The Language Instinct*, reads, "To a scientist, the fundamental fact of human language is its sheer improbability." Do you include both the author and the page within parentheses? It depends. In MLA style, the following is acceptable:

> One prominent linguist points out that "to a scientist, the fundamental fact of human language is its sheer improbability" (Pinker 371).

But so is the following:

> The linguist Steven Pinker points out that "to a scientist, the fundamental fact of human language is its sheer improbability" (371).

What is the difference? The first example refers to Pinker simply as a "prominent linguist," whereas the second refers to Pinker by name. Because the second sentence already identifies Pinker, you don't need to put his name in the parentheses; that would violate the rule of concision.

Neither parentheses uses the title of Pinker's book or his first name; you would only include these if not including them would violate the rule of precision. For example, you would include a short version of Pinker's book title if your Works Cited (the MLA name for a bibliography) also contained a different work by Steven Pinker, and you would include his first name if your Works Cited also contained a work by a different author named Pinker.

All styles seek to follow these principles. Why does MLA bibliography follow the author's name with the title, while APA follows the author name with the year of publication? Because these are the ways the two styles distinguish among multiple items by a single author (precision). Why does MLA use short titles, rather than whole titles, in parenthetical references? Because only part of the title will provide sufficient distinguishing information (concision). And so forth. Of course, no citation system is perfect; you can always find ambiguous cases. Moreover, each system has its specific requirements: in APA, for example, you *always* include the publication year in parentheses even if only one source was cited. Finally, the Internet and related technologies keep creating new ways to store information, and so every system is evolving to keep up with reality. But if you understand these two principles, a lot of what seems arbitrary about a particular citation system may start to make more sense.

Ways of Citing

You should cite other writers' words when they capture an idea, concept, or turn of phrase that you want to introduce in your writing. This is a way to bring other perspectives into your writing, introduce ideas that support or challenge your thinking, and refer to the texts that have brought you to a particular interpretation.

Quoting—using a source's words and structure exactly as they appear—is the most obvious way to cite a source, but quotations are not the only way you can integrate others' ideas into your paper. Other methods include paraphrasing and summarizing, which involve putting a source's information into your own words.

Use quotation marks to signal to readers that you are using another writer's exact words in your writing. Use a quotation when you want to introduce another voice into your text or when you find a writer making a point so eloquently that you need to reproduce that exact wording in your work.

When you quote, follow these steps: *introduce* the source (naming, most likely, the title of the text you are quoting from and the writer's name and expert status); bring in the actual quotation (and how you format this depends on the length of what you quote); *cite* the quotation by stating the writer's name and the page number you are quoting in parentheses; and *explain* the quotation.

Making these moves—introduce, citing, and explaining quotations—will help you transition between your writing and others', and it will help situate quotations in your texts. This approach is often referred to as **I–C–E**; you'll want to be sure to **I–C–E** both your quotations and paraphrases.

Paraphrasing allows you to acknowledge others' ideas and arguments in your work without drawing on their actual words. You still introduce the writer and the text you are working with, draw from their writing while putting their thoughts in your own words, and cite the source by providing the writer's name and the page number where the idea or concept appears in their work.

When you want to refer to a piece of writing in a more general way, when you need to point to an argument a writer makes throughout a text, or want to introduce a piece before you move on to work with it more closely, you will summarize. When you summarize a text, you provide an overview of it by giving your readers a general idea of what the text is about. Strong summaries are short and provide a sense of what is central to the text you are summing up.

By quoting, paraphrasing, and summarizing other texts, you join larger, ongoing conversations; you take your turn in such text-based conversations by responding to others as you introduce your own ideas through your writing.

When Not to Cite

You do not have to cite when you present an idea, concept, or turn of phrase that is commonly known. *Common knowledge*—knowledge that your readers will most likely be familiar with—does not have to be cited in your writing. While the actual definition of common knowledge is a bit arbitrary and hard to pin down, you should ask yourself if you are presenting a new or unfamiliar idea to your readers. If so, cite it in your writing. Remember, citing helps you show your readers what you've read and that you are familiar with the larger conversation you are entering. Careful and complete citations show that your writing is credible and worth reading.

Many students think that they cite only written texts such as books and articles. The truth is that academic writers cite many other kinds of texts, including images, videos, and songs. Further, some students think they must cite only when they quote someone's words directly. In fact, you must cite *whenever* you rely on another person's words, ideas, or information. Citation, in other words, is a complex business.

Quote, Paraphrase, or Summarize?

Think about your reasons for citing a source. Are you mainly interested in the author's *language*? You may cite a work because its author expresses something in a memorable way. In these cases, you will probably want to cite by means of quotation.

Are you mainly interested in the author's *idea*? If the ideas are more important than the language, or if it benefits your paper to put the author's ideas in your own words, then you will probably want to paraphrase.

Are you mainly interested in the *information* in the source? If you are citing a scientific text, for example, and you want to cite the basic numerical result from that text, your citation will probably take the form of a summary. (Even though you may use the exact numbers as your source, citations of data are not usually in quotation marks.)

In short, your decision to quote, paraphrase, or summarize depends on your reasons for citing. It also depends on the field of your writing. For example, literature papers tend to quote a lot because they are, almost by definition, focused on the language of texts. Scientific papers, on the other hand, almost never quote because they are focused on ideas and information.

Increasing Your Citation Sophistication

Because most students learn to cite in English classes, they learn citation as a matter of quoting. Therefore, most students, when they first start citing sources, tend to cite only work that supports their point. Later, as they became more confident in their own ideas and more willing to engage with other writers and thinkers, some students learn how to disagree with others—even with published writers. Later still, some learn to adopt the most complex, sophisticated position of all, one in which you may agree in some ways and disagree with others in a text.

Figure 2 shows one way of visualizing these possibilities: the reasons for citing (language, idea, and information) and the ways of interacting (agreement, disagreement, or both). Make a few photocopies of this figure. The next time you write using citations, place an X in the appropriate box each time you cite a source. Do the citations tend to cluster toward the top left of the diagram, only quoting and only in agreement? On the whole, a paper that uses citations well will tend to have citations distributed throughout the grid.

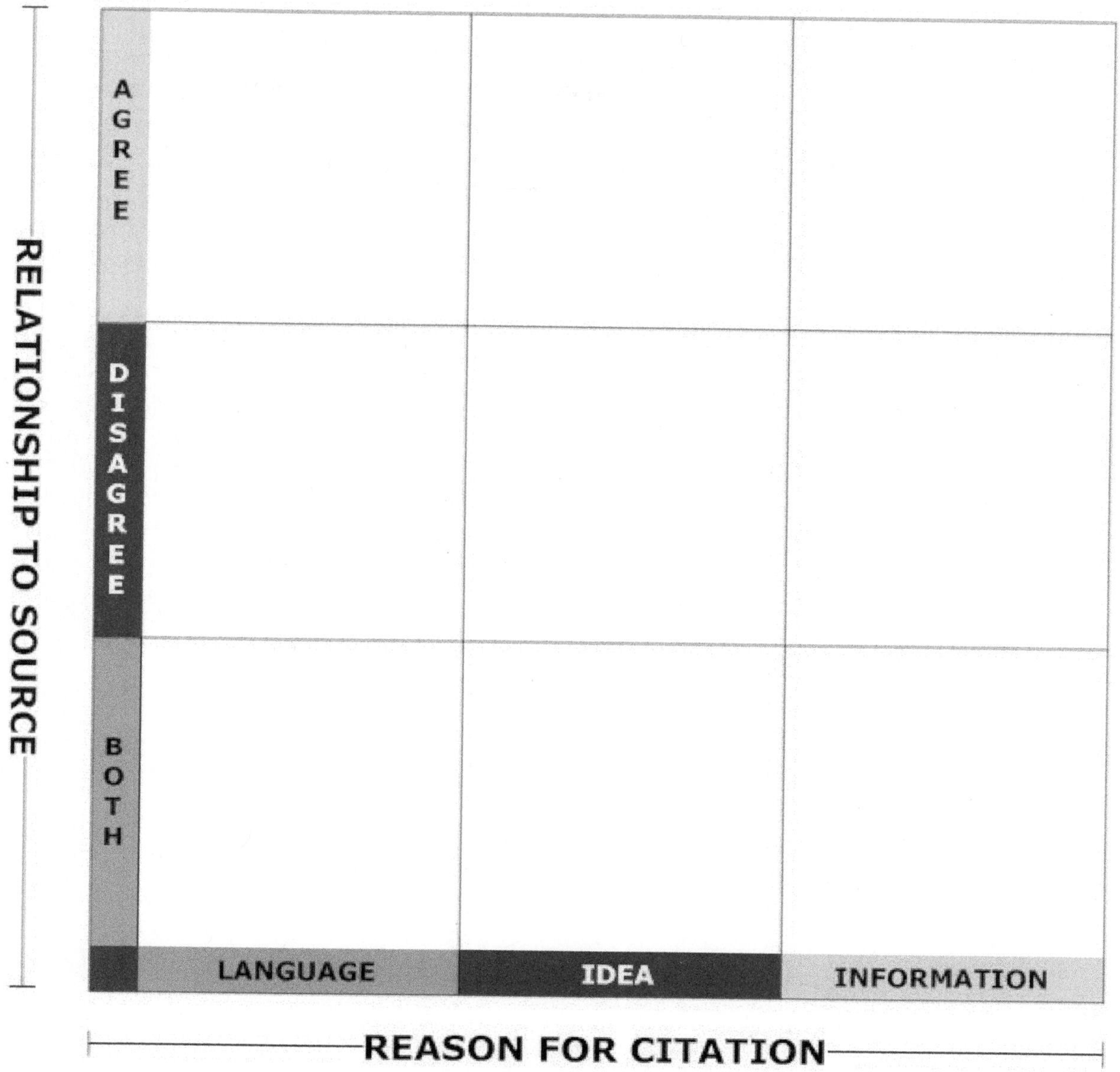

Figure 2: The Citation Matrix. Use this figure to track why you cite (for reasons of language, idea, or information) and how you relate to each citation (agreement, disagreement, or both). Put an X in the appropriate box for each time you cite. A well-written paper that uses many sources will have X's scattered across the diagram.

Conclusion: Citation as a Practice

At the beginning of this chapter, we defined citation as a *practice* and a *habit* of academic writers. Of course you (and your teachers) will want you to cite in ways that are correct for each class. True mastery of citation, however, is not just mastery of a particular citation style. Rather, it is an understanding of citation that you can adapt to new circumstances. With practice in ENGL 101 and 102, you can learn the principles of citation in such a way that, faced with *any* citation style, you have the mental and behavioral tools to tackle the problem with relative ease.

Using the Modern Language Association (MLA) Style

How Do I Format My Paper According to MLA Style?

MLA style requires that you number all pages (including the first page) in the upper-right corner of the page one-half inch from the top and put your last name before the page number. Your margins are one inch on the right and left sides; a heading (with your name, your instructor's name, the course number and section number, and the date of submission) is included one inch from the top of the page in the left corner. The essay is double-spaced throughout, including the Works Cited page. The title of your essay is centered one double-space below the header and one double-space above the first line of your introductory paragraph. The first line of every paragraph is indented one-half inch (or one TAB).

Here is what a paper that follows MLA format looks like:

Last Name 1

Name

Dr. Instructor

ENGL 101*01

1 May 2011

Centered Essay Title

  The essay begins here, indented one TAB or half-inch. The font for this essay is 12-point Times New Roman, the default setting. The margins for this essay are one inch on each side. Notice that this essay is in normal text (not bold or underlined). Capitalize the first letter of each word in the title except prepositions and articles, unless the preposition or article begins the title, such as the title "The Life and Times of a Composition Student."

How Do I Cite Using Parenthetical Citations?

To bring readers into a quotation and move smoothly between your voice and the voice of another writer, you should introduce quotations. Do this by providing the author's name and/or the title of the text you are quoting before you provide quotation marks and bring in the actual quotation. At the end of a quotation, provide the page or paragraph number in the parentheses. (See the "Author's name in text" example.)

Your parenthetical citation should give enough information to identify the source as it is listed in your Works Cited. If you have two or more authors with the same last name, you need to use first initials or first names of the authors as well, e.g., (A. Strickland 709). If you use more than one work from the same author, you need to include a shortened title for the particular work from which you are quoting, e.g., (Gill *How Starbucks* 13).

The following are some of the most common examples of parenthetical citations.

1. Author's name in text

When you provide an author's name in introducing a quotation, include only a page number in parentheses. It is also helpful to provide some information about this writer to establish credibility.

Example. Audrey Jaffe, author of "Spectacular Sympathy: Visuality and Ideology in Dickens' *A Christmas Carol*," says, "A narrative whose ostensible purpose is the production of social sympathy, *A Christmas Carol* resembles those scenes in eighteenth-century fiction in which encounters between charity givers and receivers offer readers a model of sympathy" (329). The cultural norm of givers and receivers is amplified in *A Christmas Carol*.

2. Author's name in reference

At other times, you will not name the author in your signal phrase; in these cases, provide the author's name in the parenthetical citation. If the work you are referencing has no author, use a shortened version of the work's title to refer directly to the name that begins the entry in the Works Cited. The shortened version of the work's title must appear in the Works Cited entry in parentheses, and the first word of the shortened version must match the first word of the Works Cited entry.

Example. One argument states that, "A narrative whose ostensible purpose is the production of social sympathy, *A Christmas Carol* resembles those scenes in eighteenth-century fiction in which encounters between charity givers and receivers offer readers a model of sympathy" (Jaffe 329). The cultural norm of givers and receivers is amplified in *A Christmas Carol.*

3. No author given

When the source does not have an author, use the title as you would have the author's name.

Example. "Guidelines for the Ethical Treatment of Students and Student Writing in Composition Studies," published in *College Composition and Communication*, asserts that, "Although composition specialists embrace a variety of theoretical frameworks and research methodologies, they share a commitment to protecting the rights, privacy, dignity, and well-being of the students who are involved in their studies" (1).

Example. When examining the gender roles assigned the characters in *Hamlet*, it is easy to see that "For all of Gertrude's villainy, she is still a 'mere' woman" ("Blood and the Barbarian" 10).

How Do I Quote?

4. Indirect quotation

At times you may find the need to use an indirect quotation, which is a quotation you found in another source that was quoting the original. Use "qtd. in" to indicate the source.

Example. Groening has said, "I get lots of letters from teachers and college professors who have used *The Simpsons* to illustrate some point in class" (qtd. in Kristiansen, par. 9).

Note: This in-text citation shows how to format a digital source that has numbered paragraphs. This is one of the few cases when you will include a comma in an in-text citation.

5. Long or block quotations

Sometimes you'll need to use long quotations to support a point. If your quotation is prose (not poetry or verse), and longer than four typed lines in your text, omit the quotation marks and start the quotation on a new line. This is called a block quotation. It should be indented one inch from the left margin (or two TABS) throughout, should extend to the right margin, and should be double-spaced. If you are introducing the quotation with a complete sentence, as with other quotations, the sentence should end with a colon. With a block quotation, the period should be placed at the end of the quotation, before the parenthetical citation. The end punctuation is followed by the citation.

If a second paragraph is necessary, indent three additional spaces (one-quarter inch) to set the second paragraph apart from the first paragraph. Below is an example of a block quotation. The quotation is introduced, is quoted accurately, and the quotation is followed by an explanation or comment.

Note: Many instructors do not allow block quotations (or more than one block quotation) in an essay fewer than four or five pages, so check your instructor's policy before using one.

Example.

David W. Orr asks a series of rhetorical questions to encourage readers to see environmental issues from the perspective of people who will live after us:

> What will [future generations] think about the policy decisions we're making today? Will they applaud the precision of cost-benefit calculations that discount their prospects? Will they think us prudent for delaying action until even the most minute scientific doubts have been erased? Will they admire our stubborn devotion to inefficient vehicles, urban sprawl, and fossil-fuel consumption? Hardly. (409)

Viewed from this perspective, Orr argues, no other consideration seems as important as preserving the environment for the future.

Note: In this example, notice that no quotation marks are used, the block quotation is double-spaced, and the period comes before the parenthetical documentation. Also, this block quotation is both introduced and explained. The [bracket] used shows that the writer also added language to this quotation. Finally, note that the explanation of the quotation starts on the next line but does not start a new paragraph.

6. Replaced or added words in a quotation

If you need to add words to a quotation to clarify its meaning or to make a sentence grammatically correct, put brackets around the words you add to indicate that they are not part of the original text. For accuracy's sake, be sure that the words do not change the original meaning of the text.

Example.

Source: "With some episodes, just a page synopsis is attached; with others a full script may accompany the videocassette. We do not know the availability of these accompanying materials" (Yochelson, par. 5).

Quotation with added word: "With some episodes, just a page synopsis is attached; with others a full script may accompany the videocassette. [Researchers] do not know the availability of these accompanying materials" (Yochelson, par. 5).

7. Omitted words from a quotation

If you find it necessary to omit words in a quotation, you should use an ellipsis—three periods in a row with spaces in between—to represent the words deleted from the sentence. If you omit more than one sentence from a quotation, the ellipsis has four periods. Never use ellipses, though, at the beginning or end of a quotation; only use them in the middle of a quotation.

Your instructor may prefer that you place brackets around any ellipsis you add to quotations, to indicate that you, and not the source, have included the ellipsis. If the quotation you're using has an ellipsis in it already, and you add an additional ellipsis, you must use brackets around the ellipsis you've added.

Note: When using ellipses, you may need to make changes to keep a sentence grammatically correct. Remember to use brackets when you do this.

Example.

Source: "Programs and other discourses of television attempt to sell us to advertisers, sell us things, tell us stories, represent the world outside our living rooms, stir our passions, amuse us, and, above all, keep us watching."

Student Text: Robert C. Allen, editor of *Channels of Discourse, Reassembled: Television and Contemporary Criticism*, writes, "Programs and other discourses of television attempt to . . . tell us stories, represent the world outside our living rooms, stir our passions, amuse us, and, above all, keep us watching" (2).

8. Citation in the middle of a sentence

Quotations do not always have to stand on their own, and some quotations actually work best if they are combined with your own words. Note how the writer transitions from his/her own words to the quotation in the following example.

Example. When it becomes obvious that "Hamlet learns nothing from either show, because Claudius doesn't react to the dumb show, or he reacts with some ambiguous giving out" (Roth 3), it can be inferred that Hamlet has yet another reason not to act.

9. Emphasizing words in a quotation

If you want to stress a word used in a quotation, you will place that word in italics. In the parenthetical citation you will add the words "emphasis added" to show that the italics were not in the original source. If the emphasis is included in the original, add "emphasis original" to your parenthetical citation.

Example. Kelly Ritter, in "The Economics of Authorship: Online Paper Mills, Student Writers, and First-Year Composition," suggests that we move beyond a view of student writing grounded only by grades by "talking with our students about the *value* of writing" (624, emphasis original).

Note: Also, if there is a grammatical problem in something you quote, you can include this inconsistency in the quotation and show your readers you are aware of it by adding sic in brackets. This allows you to preserve something that was incorrect in the original.

Citing online sources

Print sources and Internet/electronic sources are formatted differently in MLA Style. Only in the citation for an online source is there a comma between the author's last name and the paragraph number. Page numbers are not required.

10. A parenthetical citation for a website

If the creator/author of the online source numbers the paragraphs of the source, you use paragraph numbers in the parenthetical citation as follows (par. 1). Only cite the paragraph number if the author has numbered the paragraphs! If the paragraphs are not numbered by the author of the website or online source, no page or paragraph numbers should be used for online sources.

Example. "*The Simpsons* is a show satirizing every element of society and culture, but at the same time swiftly becoming part of the cultural heritage of the culture it is mocking" (Kristiansen, par. 1).

11. Quotation from consecutive pages

Quotations that continue from one page to the next should be quoted accurately, and should have the name of the author and the page numbers in parentheses.

Example. "The audience hears only a fleeting, secondhand reference to this report, emphasizing its tenuous nature. We as audience get unambiguous confirmation of the murder, and Claudius' guilt" (Roth 1-2).

12. Two authors not named in your sentence

Many books and articles have more than one author or editor. To cite a book with multiple authors, include both or all of their names.

Example. (Baker and Kences 159-189)

13. Citing several works

If you are synthesizing or quoting more than one source into a paragraph, cite each author/work as you normally would and use semicolons to separate each source citation.

Example. (Kirszner 947; Lugo 12; Roth 22)

Creating a Works Cited Page

The Works Cited page appears at the end of your paper. It is vital to your paper, as it provides the information necessary for others to locate and read any sources you cite in your text. Each source you use in your essay must appear in your Works Cited, and each source in your Works Cited must have been cited in the text of your essay—no exceptions. Sources are listed in alphabetical order by the author's last name (if no author's name is provided, see the fifth point below). Do not number or bullet the entries. Your header (containing your last name and page number) should appear on your Works Cited page as well.

→ The Works Cited should begin on a separate page at the end of your essay. The Works Cited page has 1 inch margins on all sides and a header with your last name and the page number 0.5 inches from the top just like all the other pages of your paper. This page should have the title Works Cited centered at the top of the page (with no italics, quotation marks, or underlining).

→ The first line of each entry is typed flush to the left margin. If the entry is too long to fit on one line, each subsequent line should be indented one-half inch, or one tab to form a hanging indent. Most word processing programs have a hanging indent function. Using this function rather than the tab key helps prevent your text being arbitrarily moved about should alterations to the citation need to be made.

→ Double-space your Works Cited, just as you formatted your paper. Do not include extra spaces between entries.

→ Alphabetize the Works Cited by the first major word in each entry (by the author's last name or the first word of the title). Do not use articles—"a," "an," or "the"—for determining the alphabetical order.

→ If a cited work does not have an author, alphabetize by the title of the work, using a shortened version of the title in the in-text parenthetical citation if the title is too long.

→ If a cited work begins with a number (such as "100 Greatest Movies of All Time"), alphabetize the number as if it were written out (so, imagine "100…" as "One hundred"). Keep the number, but position it on the Works Cited page as if it was spelled out.

→ Author's names are given with the last name first, e.g., Harris, Emmylou. If a work has more than one author, invert the first author's name only, follow it with a comma, and then continue listing the rest of the authors.

→ If you have cited more than one work by the same author, order the works alphabetically by title, and use three hyphens in place of the author's name for every entry after the first.

→ Generally, capitalize each word in the titles of articles, books, films, songs, and other works. This rule does not apply to conjunctions, short prepositions or articles unless one of these is the first word of the title or subtitle (e.g., *They Say, I Say: The Moves That Matter in Academic Writing*).

→ Place quotation marks around the titles of articles in newspapers, magazines, journals, and webpages, as well as short stories, book chapters, songs, poems, and individual episodes of a television series.

→ Italicize the titles of independently published texts, such as books, journals, magazines, newspapers, films, television shows, album or CD titles, and works of visual art (paintings, sculptures, photos, etc).

→ For works with more than one edition, give the edition number and the abbreviation for edition directly after the title of the work (e.g., *First-Year Composition Guide*. 3rd ed.).

→ If you do not have access to certain information (e.g., the author of a website, the date of posting, or the corporate sponsor) leave it out; however, be sure to do adequate research to try to find this information.

The list below provides some commonly used citations.

Forms for print sources

MLA requires that print sources be identified by placing the word "Print" at the end of the citation (see below for examples).

1.   Books (Includes Brochures, Pamphlets, and Graphic Novels)

Provide the author's last name, followed by his/her first name. *Title*. The city of publication: Publisher, the year of publication. Type of medium—print or web. Indent
any second lines one tab.

Moore, Alan. *The Watchmen*. Absolute ed. Illus. Dave Gibbons. New York: DC Comics,
2005. Print.

Pally, Marcia. *Sex & Sensibility: Reflections on Forbidden Mirrors and the Will to Censor*. Hopewell, NJ: Ecco, 1984. Print.

2.   Books with Two or More Authors

Author's name, and second author's name. *Title of Book*. Place of publication: Publisher,
date of publication. Print.

Douglas, Kym, and Cindy Pearlman. *The Black Book of Hollywood Diet Secrets*. New
York: Plume, 2007. Print.

Note: A comma is used between the author's names even if there are only two
authors.

3.   **Two Books by the Same Author**

Use three dashes in place of the author's name in the consecutive entries. Be sure the entries are in alphabetical order (excluding articles).

Sedaris, David. *Dress Your Family in Corduroy and Denim*. New York: Back Bay Books, 2004. Print.

—. *Me Talk Pretty One Day*. New York: Back Bay Books, 2001. Print.

4.   **Chapter from a Book**

Author(s) of the chapter. "Title of the Chapter in Quotes with All Important Words Capitalized." *Title of the Book*. Ed. followed by the name of the editor in standard name order. City of publication: Publisher, Date. Page numbers of chapter. Print.

Powell, Pegeen Reichert. "Interventions at the Intersections: An Analysis of Public Writing and Student Writing." *Writing against the Curriculum: Anti-Disciplinary in the Writing and Cultural Studies Classroom*. Ed. Randi Gray Kristensen and Ryan M. Claycomb. Lanham: Lexington Books, 2010. 57-72. Print.

5.   **Anthology or Collection**

Editor's name(s), ed. *Title of Book*. City of publication: Publisher, date. Print.

Smith, Allison D., Trixie G. Smith, and Karen Wright. *COMPbiblio: Leaders and Influences in Composition Theory and Practice*. Southlake, TX: Fountainhead, 2007. Print.

6.   A Work in an Anthology

Author's name. "The Title of the Text with All Important Words Capitalized." *The Title of the Anthology in Italics.* The name(s) of the editors. The city of publication: Publisher, the year of publication. The pages used. Type of medium—print or web.

Place, J.A., and L.S. Peterson. "Some Visual Motifs of Film Noir." *Movies and Methods.* Ed. Bill Nichols. Berkley: University of California Press, 1976. 325-38. Print.

7.   More Than One Text from the Same Anthology

Students often find it necessary to use multiple sources from the same anthology in an assignment. Rather than providing a full citation from the same anthology you may bundle the texts.

Provide the editor(s) name. *The Title of the Anthology in Italics.* City of publication: Publisher, the year of publication. Type of medium—print or web.

Then, create an abbreviated citation for each individual text from the anthology used by starting a new entry using the author's last name, the title of the text in quotes, the editor(s) last name and the page numbers.

Lunsford, Andrea, et al. *Everyone's an Author.* New York: Norton, 2012. Print.

Brideau, Jan. "Lydia's Story." Lunsford et al. 128-131.

Denby, David. "Out of the West: Clint Eastwood's Shifting Landscape." Lunsford et al. 256-259.

Havrilesky, Heather. "*Mad Men:* Stillbirth of the American Dream." Lunsford et al 170-175.

Herbert, Bob. "Our Schools Must Do Better." Lunsford et al. 89-91.

8.   Article in a Reference Book

Author's name. "Title of Essay/Entry with All Important Words Capitalized." *Title of Collection*. Ed. Editor's Name(s). City of Publication: Publisher, year. Page range of entry. Medium of Publication.

Harris, Muriel. "Talk to Me: Engaging Reluctant Writers." *A Tutor's Guide: Helping Writers One to One*. Ed. Ben Rafoth. Portsmouth, NH: Heinemann, 2000. 24-34. Print.

9.   Article in a Scholarly Journal

Author's name. "Title of the Article with All Important Words Capitalized." *Journal Title* volume number. Issue number (date of publication): pages. Print.

Aleksiuk, Natasha. "'A Thousand Angles': Photographic Irony in the Work of Julia Margaret Cameron and Virginia Woolf." *Mosaic* 33.2 (2000): 125-42. Print.

10.   Article in a Scholarly Journal that Uses Only Issue Numbers

Author's name. "Title of the Article with All Important Words Capitalized." *Journal Title* issue number (date of publication): pages. Print.

Avery, Todd. "'The Girls in Europe is Nuts Over Ball Players': Ring Lardner and Virginia Woolf." *Nine* 13 (2005): 31-53. Print.

11.   Newspaper Article

Author's name. "Title of Article with All Important Words Capitalized." *Newspaper Title* day month year: pages. Print.

Taylor, Mark C. "End the University as We Know It." *The New York Times* 26 Apr. 2009: A23. Print.

12.   Review

Reviewer's name. "Title of Review with All Important Words Capitalized." Rev. of *Title of Work*, by name of author (editor, director, etc.). *Journal* day month year: pages. Medium of Publication.

Ebert, Roger. "A Monosyllabic Superhero Who Wouldn't Pass the Turing Test." Rev. of *X-Men Origins: Wolverine*, by Dir. Gavin Hood. *Chicago Sun-Times* 29 Apr. 2009: E4. Print.

13.   Religious Works

Title of Work. Name of editor. Place of publication: Publisher, date. Print.

The Holy Bible: King James Version. Thomas Nelson Bibles. Nashville: Thomas Nelson, 2004. Print.

Note: You can give the title of the book within the Bible as well as chapter and verse information in your parenthetical citation (e.g., The Holy Bible Genesis 1:1 or Koran 7.3).

Forms for online sources

Every work cited entry must include a media marker, such as *print* or *web*. For online sources, use the word 'Web' just before the Date of Access at the end of the bibliographic entry. Using the URL is not required. An exception to this is that you may need to include it after the "Date of Access" in angle brackets if your source cannot be easily found by typing the author and title into a search engine or if your professor requires it.

14. Web Site

Author's name. *Name of Web Site*. Institution or organization associated with/producing the website. Date of posting/revision. Web. Date of access.

Swan, Mike. *BRAT Online*. Basenji Rescue and Transport. 2009. Web. 20 Apr. 2009.

The Virginia Woolf Society of Great Britain. Apr. 2005. Web. 6 Mar. 2006.

15. Article on a Web Site

Author's name. "Article Title with All Important Words Capitalized." *Name of Web Site*. Name of institution or organization associated with/producing the Web site. Date of posting/revision. Web. Date of access.

Carroll, Jason. "Homeless Asked to Pay Rent." *CNN.com*. 10 May 2009. Web. 11 May 2009.

16. Online Newspaper or Magazine Author's name.

Author's name. "Title of Article with All Important Words Capitalized." *Newspaper Title* day month year: pages. Web. Date of access.

Atlas, Darla, et al. "Life in the Cult." *People* 28 Apr. 2008: 62-7. Web. 20 Apr. 2009.

17. Online Journal Article

Author's name. "Title of Article." *Title of Journal* Vol. Issue (Year): pages. Web. Date of access.

Gill, R. B. "Kerouac and the Comic Dilemma." *Studies in Popular Culture* 27.3 (2004): 87-98. Web. 12 Apr. 2009.

18. Article from an Online Database (such as General OneFile, LexisNexis, Academic Search Premier, or JSTOR)

Author's name. "Title of the Article." *Journal Title* vol. issue (date of publication): pages. *Name of Database or Other Relevant Information*. Web. Date of access.

Bellamy, Alex J. "Dirty Hands and Lesser Evils in the War on Terror." *British Journal of Politics & International Relations* 9.3 (Aug. 2007): 509-526. *Academic Search Premier*. Web. 7 May 2009.

González, Esther Sánchez-Pardo. "'What Phantasmagoria the Mind Is': Reading Virginia Woolf's Parody of Gender." *Atlantis, Revista de la Asociación Española de Estudios Anglo- Norteamericanos* 26.2 (2004): 75-86. *InfoTrac OneFile*. Web. 4 March 2006.

Lavelle, Ellen, and Nancy Zuercher. "The Writing Approaches of University Students." *Higher Education* 42.3 (2001): 373-391. *JSTOR*. Web. 18 May 2010.

19. Newspaper Article Accessed through *Access World News*

Author's name. "Title of the Article with All Important Words Capitalized." *Newspaper Title* date of publication: pages. *Name of Database or Other Relevant Information*. Access Provider. Web. Date of access.

McManus, Doyle. "The Cost of Killing by Remote Control." *Los Angeles Times* 4 May 2009: A13. *NewsBank Access World News*. Web. 7 May 2009.

20.   Article Accessed through *CQ Researcher*

Author's name. "Title of the Article with All Important Words Capitalized." *Periodical Title* volume number. Issue number (Date of Publication): pages. *Name of Database*. Web. Date of access.

Clemmitt, Marcia. "Extreme Sports." *CQ Researcher* 19.13 (2009): 297-320. *CQ Researcher Online*. Web. 7 May 2009.

21.   Article Accessed through *Opposing Viewpoints*

Author's name. "Title of the Article with All Important Words Capitalized." *Name of Viewpoint.* Editor. City of Publication: Publisher, date of publication. *Name of Database*. Web. Date of access.

Marable, Manning. "Slavery Reparations Would Promote Social Justice." *Social Justice.* Ed. William Dudley. San Diego: Greenhaven Press, 2005. *Opposing Viewpoints In Context*. Web. 7 May 2009.

22. Electronic Book

Author's name. *Title of the Book.* City of Publication: Publisher, date of publication. Name of database. Web. Date of access.

Heymann, Jody, Joshua Cohen, and Joel Rogers. *Can Working Families Ever Win?* Boston: Beacon Press, 2002. NetLibrary. Web. 7 May 2009.

23. Magazine Article with an Author

Author's name. "Title of Article with All Important Words Capitalized." *The Title of the Magazine in Italics.* Name of database. Web. Date you accessed the article.

Borowitz, Andy. "Emily Dickinson, Jerk of Amherst." *New Yorker* 74.35 (1998): 48.

   Academic Search Premier. Web. 27 Jan 2011.

24.   Magazine Article without an Author

"Title of the Article with All Important Words Capitalized." *The Name of the Magazine in Italics.* The issue date: page(s). Publisher. Name of Datebase. Type of medium. The date accessed you personally accessed the article.

"Emily Dickinson Came to Earth and Then She Left." *Nation.* Nov. 2010: 33. Nation

   Company, L.P. *Academic Search Premier.* Web. 27 Jan 2011.

Forms for other commonly used sources

Since all entries must include a media marker, identify the actual broadcast medium for other commonly used sources (see below for examples).

25.   Dictionary Definition

"Term you define." Def. # (to show which definition you are citing). *Dictionary Title.* Ed.

   Date of Publication. Print.

"Reflect." Def. 1b. *The Oxford English Dictionary.* 2nd ed. 1989. Print.

You might be citing an online dictionary; if so, make sure to note that medium.

"Empowerment." *Oxford English Dictionary Online.* 2nd ed. 1989. Web. 15 May 2011.

If the entry you are citing is one among several for the same word, add "Entry" and the appropriate definition number (or designation).

"Honor." Entry 1. Def. 8a. *Merriam-Webster Online Dictionary.* 1989. Web. 12 Feb.

   2011.

26.   Television or Radio Program

"Title of Episode or Segment with All Important Words Capitalized." *Title of Program or Series*. Name of network. Call letters and city of the local station (if applicable). Broadcast date. Medium of reception (e.g. Radio, Television). Supplemental information (e.g. Transcript).

"Man of Science, Man of Faith." *Lost*. ABC. 21 May 2005. Television.

27.   Sound Recording

Artist/Band. "Song Title." *Title of Album*. Manufacturer, year of issue. Medium (e.g. Audiocassette, CD, Audiotape, LP, Digital Download).

Wilco. "Jesus Don't Cry." *Yankee Hotel Foxtrot*. Nonesuch, 2002. CD.

28.   Liner Notes

Author's name. Description of material. *Album Title*. Manufacturer, date. Medium (e.g. Audiocassette, CD, Audiotape, LP, Digital Download).

Smashing Pumpkins. Liner Notes. *Siamese Dream*. Virgin, 1993. CD.

29.   Film

Title. Dir. Director's name. Perf. Actor's names (if relevant). Distributor, year of release. Medium.

Goodfellas. Dir. Martin Scorsese. Perf. Ray Liotta, Lorraine Bracco. Warner Bros., 1991. Film.

Note: If you are citing the contribution of one specific actor, director, writer, and so forth, you may begin the entry with that person's name (as you do with an author). You may include other data about the film, such as the names of the writer, performers, and producer, after the director's name.

30.   Advertisements

Name of Product, Company, or Institution. Descriptive label (advertisement). Then provide the usual publication information of the publication as well as the medium.

Champion: Hoodie Remix. Advertisement. *People* 10 May 2009: 40. Print.

31.   Painting, Sculpture, or Photograph

Artist's name. *Title*. Medium of Composition. Name of institution that houses the work or the individual who owns the work, city.

O'Keefe, Georgia. *Sky Above Clouds IV*. 1965. Oil on Canvas. The Art Institute of Chicago, Illinois.

Note: You may add the creation date of a work immediately after the title.

32.   Personal Interview

Name of interviewee. Descriptive Title of Interview (e.g., Personal, Telephone, Webcam). Date of interview.

Rebecca Bobbitt. Personal Interview. 1 Jan. 2009.

33.   Lecture, Speech, Address, or Reading

Author's name. "Title of Speech with All Important Words Capitalized." Location where speech was given. Date of presentation. Descriptive label (e.g., Lecture, Speech, Address, Reading).

Baldwin, Dianna. "Living a Second Life: Virtual Worlds in the Composition Classroom." First-Year Composition, English 101. Michigan State University, East Lansing. 17 October 2008. Lecture.

34. Live Performance—Play, Musical, Concert, Etc.

Name of the Play/Concert in Italics. Name of writer/composer. Name of director. Name of performer(s). Site of play/concert. Date you saw the play/concert. Performance.

The Phantom of the Opera. Music by Frank Lloyd Weber & Lyrics by Charles Hart. Dir. Harold Prince. Perf. Cris Grownendaal, Susan Cuthburt and Doug LeBrecque. Manitoba Centennial Concert Hall, Winnepeg. 23 June 1992. Performance.

35. Work of Art from an Online Source

Provide the name of the artist. *The Name of the Artistic Work in Italics*, followed by the year or circa. The name of the media type (oil painting, pastel, photograph, sculpture, etc.). The name of the location of the piece of art. *The database name*. Type of medium. Date you personally accessed the database.

Hine, Lewis. K. *Harlem Club, Pool Game*. c1923-1938. Photograph. George Eastman House. Rochester. *ARTstor*. Web. 27 Jan 2011.

36. Online Film Database

Name of the Film. The name of the production studio making the film. The year the film was released. *The name of the database*. Type of medium. The date you personally accessed the database.

Edgar Allan Poe's "The Cask of Amontillado". Films Media Group, 1998. Films On Demand. Web. 01 February 2011.

Sample Works Cited

Following is an example of a completed Works Cited placed at the end of a paper. Note that all media sources are combined and alphabetized in a single list.

Works Cited

Avery, Todd. "'The Girls in Europe Is Nuts over Ball Players': Ring Lardner and Virginia Woolf." *Nine* 13 (2005): 31-53. Print.

"Empowerment." *Oxford English Dictionary Online*. 2nd ed. 1989. Web. 15 May 2011.

Marable, Manning. "Slavery Reparations Would Promote Social Justice." *Social Justice*. Ed. William Dudley. San Diego: Greenhaven Press, 2005. *Opposing Viewpoints Resource Center*. Gale. Web. 7 May 2009.

O'Keefe, Georgia. *Sky Above Clouds IV*. 1965. Oil on Canvas. The Art Institute of Chicago, Illinois.

Sedaris, David. *Dress Your Family in Corduroy and Denim*. New York: Back Bay Books, 2004. Print.

Wilco. "Jesus Don't Cry." *Yankee Hotel Foxtrot*. Nonesuch, 2002. CD.

What Is an Annotated Bibliography?

It is often helpful to think further about the sources you have incorporated into your text by creating an annotated bibliography. An annotated bibliography includes a correctly formatted citation, a brief summary, an analysis, and a brief evaluation of the source's value to the assignment.

Each source should be formatted as it would be on the Works Cited page—in alphabetical order, double-spaced, and with a reverse indent.

The annotation, or commentary, for each source, which will appear after each bibliographic entry, should be double-spaced. The annotation requires you to summarize, analyze and reflect on the source based on little or how great the source's value is to your research.

A. **Summarize.** What is the point of each source? What topics are covered? How would you explain this source to someone else? How would you characterize its credibility?

B. **Analyze.** What makes this source useful or not useful? Is this source biased or objective? What are the strengths and weaknesses of this source? Who else might find this source useful?

C. **Reflect.** How does this source fit into your research project? How will it help to shape your argument? If the source is not helpful or credible, how can you tell? How does it compare with other sources in your bibliography?

Example:

Battenhouse, Roy W. "Hamlet's Apostrophe on Man: Clue to the Tragedy." *PMLA* 66. 6. (1951): 1073-1113. *JSTOR*. Web. 9 Jun 2011.

Battenhouse's text deals primarily with the question: is Hamlet a character truly focused on revenge, and, if he is focused on revenge, is revenge an acceptable solution based on religious tradition or is revenge a societal condition which will put Hamlet's soul in jeopardy? Battenhouse focuses on the question Hamlet asks (To be or not to be…?) and the comments he makes about humanity in general (What a piece of work is man!) to himself and the audience. In his article, Battenhouse discusses the ways the questions and comments made by the characters are based on modern, as opposed to classical religious dogma. Battenhouse writes that *Hamlet* the play, and Hamlet the character, is placed more securely in modern religious contexts because of Hamlet's conflict with what action feels right when compared to what is biblically acceptable. The article does not provide definitive answers into why Hamlet fails to exact revenge but does offer numerous connections to the work of other researchers, which will provide several avenues for additional research. While most of Battenhouse's article does not apply specifically to the research on my topic—why Hamlet fails to seek revenge on his uncle immediately after the ghost's visit—it does offer some explanation on why Hamlet only acts when he is drawn into his uncle's trap.

The material presented in this chapter is not designed to be the only way to complete an assignment. It is a starting point. Each professor brings to the classroom his/her own assignments and his/her own methods for presenting the background material necessary to help students become successful members of the academic discourse community.

Using American Psychological Association (APA) Style

Another common academic writing system that you may encounter is APA. This style is often used in social science fields, such as psychology and sociology, as well as in many education and business courses. Some first-year composition instructors ask their students to write in APA format for one or more assignments in order to prepare them for later courses in which they will be required to write in APA style.

While there are some important differences between MLA and APA, the two styles share the same overall goals of citing and documenting source material clearly and formatting your writing in an accessible and uniform way.

Similarities to MLA

In many ways, APA formatting is similar to MLA, including the following guidelines:

- Use 12 pt. Times New Roman font throughout the paper

- Set one-inch margins on all sides

- Double-space every page of the paper (with no extra spacing between paragraphs)

- Insert page numbers in the upper-right-hand corner of each page

- Cite and document sources in two ways:

  ○ In parentheses inside the paper

  ○ In a list of sources (alphabetized by author) at the end of the paper

However, there are a number of important differences between the two systems, so please read this chapter closely to be sure that you are following APA style closely if your instructor requires you to use APA.

Elements of an APA Paper

An APA style paper is comprised of four separate parts:

- Title page

- Abstract

- Main text of the paper

- List of references (similar to a Works Cited list in MLA)

PLEASE NOTE: An instructor may choose not to require all of the above. Consult your assignment sheet and/or your instructor to be sure which parts are required for any given assignment.

Title Page

A properly-formatted title page will look like this:

Running Head: SHORTENTED TITLE OF THE PAPER   1
Full Title of the Paper: Including Subtitle If a Subtitle Is Used
Author's Name
Author's Institution (for example: Coastal Carolina University)

PLEASE NOTE: APA format requires that the words "Running Head" and a colon precede the header (the shortened title) on page one, but on all subsequent pages, you should only have the header (not including the words "Running Head" or the colon). In MS Word (2013 version), you can use the page numbering feature to insert both the header and page. Follow these directions:

7. Go to the INSERT tab.

8. Select the "Page Number" option in the "Header & Footer" section.

9. Choose the "Top of Page" option.

10. Select "Plain Number 3" to put the first page number in the upper-right-hand corner.

11. Hit the Tab key twice to move the header to the left-hand margin.

12. Type in the header you plan to use throughout the paper (that is, the header without the words "Running Head." Make sure to type the header in all capitals.

13. With your cursor still in the header section, go to the DESIGN tab.

14. Select the "Different First Page" option. (You will notice that the header will disappear from page one when you select this option.)

15. Enter the page number and the first-page header (with the words "Running Head" and a colon) on page one using steps 1-5 above.

If you have trouble formatting your title page, headers, and page numbers, you can do a quick Google search for tips on this topic. If you still have trouble after a Google search, you should consider visiting the CCU Writing Center in Kearns 203 for one-on-one assistance.

Abstract

Your instructor may require you to include an abstract for your paper. If so, please make sure to include the abstract on its own page and format it like this:

SHORTENED TITLE OF PAPER   2

Abstract

An abstract is a brief summary of your paper (typically between 150 and 250 words).

The abstract should contain all of the major ideas in your paper, but not minor details.

An abstract introduces readers to your paper and helps them decide if they want to

read all of it.

PLEASE NOTE: The abstract is always double-spaced, like all other parts of the paper, but the first line of the abstract is not indented.

Main Text of the Paper

In a paper with a title page and an abstract, the main text of the paper will begin on a new page after the abstract. The body of the paper should be formatted as shown below:

SHORTENED TITLE OF PAPER 3

Full Title of Paper: Including Subtitle if a Subtitle is Used

The introduction of the paper begins here, indented one tab (or a half inch). However, the introduction section is not labeled with a heading. Instead, the text of the paper begins with the complete title of the paper, which is centered at the top of the page (just below the header). Subsequent sections may have headings. Only the References page will need to begin on its one, separate page.

The font for the paper is Times New Roman, 12 point. The margins for the paper are one inch on all sides. The entire paper should be double-spaced with no extra spacing between paragraphs.

PLEASE NOTE: To set double spacing correctly in MS Word (2013 version), follow these steps:

16. Go to the HOME tab.

17. Click on the down arrow in the lower-right-hand corner of the "Paragraph" section.

18. Select the "Double" option under "Line spacing."

19. Click the box marked "Don't add space between paragraphs of the same style."

If you have trouble setting the line spacing in your paper, you can do a quick Google search for tips on this topic. If you still have trouble after a Google search, you should consider visiting the CCU Writing Center in Kearns 203 for one-on-one assistance.

List of References

In APA format, the list of sources used in the paper is called "References." (In MLA, this list is called "Works Cited.") The References list begins on its own page at the end of the main text. As in MLA format, the sources are listed in alphabetical order according to the author's last name. If there is no author for a source, alphabetize the source by the first word in the title.

A properly-formatted References list will look like this:

References   10

Babcock, R.D. & Thonus, T. (2012). *Researching the Writing Center: Towards*

and Evidence-Based Practice. New York: Lang.

Driscoll, D.L. & Perdue, S.W. (2012). Theory, lore, and more: An analysis of

RAD research in *The Writing Center Journal*. *Writing Center Journal*,

32(2): 11-39.

North, S.M. (1984). Writing center research: Testing our assumptions. In G.

Olson (Ed.), *Writing centers: Theory and administration*. Urbana, IL:

NCTE. 24-35.

PLEASE NOTE: The above list of references only includes a few types of sources (a book, a journal article, and a book chapter). Consult the "Creating References" section later in this chapter for detailed instructions on how to format citations for multiple types of print and online sources on your References page.

Inserting Parenthetical Citations

As in MLA, authors of your sources can be cited in the main text of your paper either in **signal phrases** at or near the beginning of a sentence or parenthetically afterwards. Both in the text and in **parenthetical citations**, only last names are used in APA format. Also, APA papers use author–date citations (as opposed to the author–page citations in MLA format) with the publication year, not the page number, always included in a parenthesis.

If you give the author's name in a signal phrase, a properly-formatted APA citation would look like this:

Although many economists favor a single-payer model, Smith (2005) claims that adopting such a system would bankrupt the federal government.

Without a signal phrase, the citation would look like this:

> Although many economists favor a single-payer model, one recent study claims that adopting such a system would bankrupt the federal government (Smith, 2005).

Dates are important in APA style because APA style was developed for the social sciences, and science is concerned with providing the most current information possible. When no date is given, write "n.d."

PLEASE NOTE:

20. Although APA is known as an author-year format as opposed to an author-page number format, it is not true that page numbers are never given in APA-style citations. In fact, page number must be given for direct quotations (after a "p." for a single page or "pp." for multiple pages). When you include a quotation in a sentence, a correct citation will look like this:

> Although many economists favor a single-payer model, one study found that "bankruptcy at the federal level would be almost certain within five years" (Smith, 2005, p. 115).

21. As in the above example the period always goes after the final parenthesis if the sentences ends in a parenthetical citation.

1. Two authors

In signal phrase. Spell out *and* between the authors' names, followed by the year in parentheses:

Example. Redelmeier and Tibshirani (1997) identify "no safety advantage to hands-free as compared with hand-held telephones" (p. 456).

In parenthetical citation. In parentheses, give both authors' names, separated by "&" (not spelled out as *and*), followed by a comma, the year, and the page number if necessary:

Example. The study identifies "no safety advantage to hands-free as compared with hand-held telephones" (Redelmeier & Tibshirani, 1997, p. 456).

2. Three to five authors

First reference. Use all authors' names, whether in the signal phrase or the parenthetical citation.

Example. Drews, Yazdani, Godfrey, Cooper, and Strayer (2009) warn us of the danger, but don't emphasize that this is from a condition of no distraction. Under actual circumstances, distractions are already present.

Example. A later study characterizes preliminary works as "seminal" (Drews, Yazdani, Godfrey, Cooper, & Strayer, 2009, p.1).

Subsequent references. For later references to a work you have already referenced, do not list all authors; instead, give the first author followed by no comma and "et al." (meaning "and others").

Example. Drews et al. (2009) maintain even off-topic work in the field has proven valuable, as there cannot not be too much data from which to draw conclusions.

Example. A later study characterizes preliminary works as "seminal" (Drews et al., 2009, p.1), as they set the bar for all subsequent research.

3. Six or more authors

Only the first author is given, even on the first reference, followed by "et al.", with no comma in between.

Example. Dehaene et al. (2010) explain the networks in the cortex and how changes in those networks can be read to reflect influence of use of technology.

4. Author's name not given

Use the leftmost portion of the entry as it appears in the list of references at the end of the paper. Usually this is the title (but it might also be a corporate author).

Example. "Assortative Mating" (2012) indicates the term assortative pairing as an alternative name for the phenomenon.

Note: Even though the title is in quotation marks in the body of the paper, it will not be inside quotation marks in the list of references at the end.

5. Indirect sources

These are acknowledged parenthetically in APA as they are in MLA, but use the phrase "as cited in" in place of "qtd. in".

Example. Research (Redelmeier & Tibshirani, 1997, as cited in Drews et al., 2009) forms a solid core for subsequent studies.

Creating References

Formatting Authors' Names in the List of References

1. One Author

Moore, A. (2005). *The Watchmen (Absolute ed.)*. New York: DC Comics.

2. Two Authors

Use last names, initials, and an ampersand (&) between them.

Redelmeier, D., & Tibshirani, R. (1997). Associations between cellular-telephone calls and motor vehicle collisions. *New England Journal of Medicine*, 336, 453-458.

PLEASE NOTE:

1. A comma is used between the author's names even if there are only two authors.

2. Always use the & symbol before the final author's name if there is more than one author.

3. No matter how the authors' names are formatted in the source, after the full last name, APA style uses only initials.

3. Three to Five Authors

Each author is specified.

Hanowski, R., Olson, R., Hickman, J., & Bocanegra, J. (2009). *Driver distraction in commercial operation* (Report no. FMCSA-RRR-09-042). Retrieved from http://www.distraction.gov /research/PDF-Files/Driver-Distraction-Commercial-Vehicle-Operations.pdf

4. Six or More Authors

For six or more authors, the first six are specified, as is the last. If there are any intervening authors, they are not listed; instead, an ellipsis (". . .") is used. So for six authors, all will be listed. For seven, all seven will be listed. But for eight and up, only the first six, an ellipsis, no &, and the last will be specified.

Dehaene, S., Pegado, F., Braga, L. W., Ventura, P., Nunes Filo, G., Jobert, A., Cohen, L. (2010, December 3). How learning to read changes the cortical networks for vision and language. *Science, 330*(6009), 1359–1364. Retrieved from http://www.sciencemag.org/content/330/6009/1359.full.pdf?sid=10c2a445-24c4-49ee-921a-2c5b04581efe

Formatting References for Print Sources

Forms for Print Sources

1. Books (Includes Brochures, Pamphlets, and Graphic Novels)

Author's last name, author's first and middle initials. (Year of publication). *Title of book.* Location: Publisher.

Pally, M. (1984). *Sex & sensibility: Reflections on forbidden mirrors and the will to censor.* Hopewell, NJ: Ecco.

2. Two or More Books by the Same Author

Use the author's name for all sources and list the sources by the year.

Sedaris, D. (2001). *Me talk pretty one day*. New York: Back Bay Books.

Sedaris, D. (2004). *Dress your family in corduroy and denim*. New York: Back Bay
Books.

3. Chapter from a Book

Author(s) of the chapter. (Year of publication). Title of chapter. In A.A. Editor & B.B. Editor (Eds.), *Title of book* (pages of chapter). Location: Publisher.

Powell, P. R. (2010). Interventions at the intersections: An analysis of public writing and
student writing. In R.G. Kristensen and R.M. Claycomb (Eds.), *Writing against
the curriculum: Anti-disciplinary in the writing and cultural studies classroom*
(pp. 57-72). Lanham: Lexington Books.

4.   Anthology or Collection

Editor(s). (Ed(s).). (Year of publication). *Title of anthology/collection*. Place of publication: Publisher.

Smith, A. D., Smith, T. G., & Wright, K. (Eds.) (2007). *COMPbiblio: Leaders and influences in composition theory and practice*. Southlake, TX: Fountainhead.

5.   A Work in an Anthology

Author(s) of the work. (Year of publication). Title of work. In A.A. Editor & B.B. Editor
(Eds.), *Title of anthology* (pages of work). Location: Publisher.

Place, J.A., & Peterson, L. S. (1976). Some visual motifs of film noir. In B. Nichols (Ed.),
Movies and methods (pp. 325-338). Berkley: University of California Press.

6. Article in a Reference Book

Author(s) of the article. (Year of publication). Title of article. In A.A. Editor & B.B. Editor (Eds.), *Title of reference* (pages of article). Location: Publisher.

Harris, M. (2000). Talk to me: Engaging reluctant writers. In B. Rafoth (Ed.), *A tutor's guide: Helping writers one to one* (pp. 24-34). Portsmouth, NH: Heinemann.

7. Article in a Scholarly Journal

Author(s) of the article. (Year, Month Day). Title of article. *Title of Periodical, volume number* (issue number), pages.

Aleksiuk, N. (2000). "A thousand angles": Photographic irony in the work of Julia Margaret Cameron and Virginia Woolf. *Mosaic, 33*(2): 25-142.

8. Newspaper Article

Author's name. (Year, Month Day). Title of article. *Newspaper Title*, p. page.

Taylor, M. C. (2009, April 26). End the university as we know it. *The New York Times*, p. A23.

9. Review

Reviewer's name. (Year, Month Day). Title of review. [Review of the work (book, film, etc.) *Title of Work*, by A.A. Author (editor, director, etc.)]. *Journal, volume*(issue), pages.

Ebert, R. (2009, April 29). A monosyllabic superhero who wouldn't pass the Turing test. [Review of the film *X-Men Origins: Wolverine*, by G. Hood]. *Chicago Sun-Times*, p. E4.

Forms for Online Sources

Only include retrieval dates if the source could change.

10. Web Site

Author(s) of site. (Year, Month Day). *Title of web site*. Retrieved Month Day, Year, from
http://Web address

Swan, M. (2013). *Basenji rescue and transport*. Retrieved April 20, 2013, from http://
www.basenjirescue.org/

The Virginia Woolf Society of Great Britain. (2005, April). Retrieved March 6, 2006, from
http://www.virginiawoolfsociety.co.uk/index.html

11. Article on a Web Site

Author(s) of article. (Year, Month Day). Title of article. *Name of web site*. Retrieved
Month Day, Year, from http://Web address

Miller, S. (2013, May 23). Dining out with food allergies. *CNN.com*. Retrieved May 23,
2013, from http://www.cnn.com/2013/05/23/health/dining-out-allergies/index.
html?hpt=he_c2

12. Article from an Online Periodical (Scholarly Journal) with a DOI [digital object identifier]

A **digital object identifier (DOI)** is an alphanumeric string assigned to an online
document that is used as a permanent link to the document's location. The string
is assigned by the International DOI Foundation, a registration agency, when an
article is published and made available online. A DOI is more reliable than an
html link, which can change over time.

Author(s). (Year, Month Day). Title of article in sentence case. *Name of Journal in Title
Case, volume*(issue), startpage–endpage. doi:10. . . .

Drews, F., Yazdani, H., Godfrey, C., Cooper, J., & Strayer, D. (2009). Text messaging during simulated driving. *Human Factors: The Journal of the Human Factors and Ergonomics Society, 51*(5), 762–770. doi:10.1177/001872080935331

13. Article from an Online Periodical (Scholarly Journal) without a DOI

Author(s). (Year, Month Day). Title of article in sentence case. *Name of Journal in Title Case, volume*(issue), startpage–endpage. Retrieved from http:// . . .

Drews, F., Yazdani, H., Godfrey, C., Cooper, J., & Strayer, D. (2009). Text messaging during simulated driving. *Human Factors: The Journal of the Human Factors and Ergonomics Society, 51*(5), 762–770. Retrieved from http://www.psych.utah.edu/ lab /appliedcognition/publications/texting.pdf

14. Article from an Online Periodical (Trade Journal) with a DOI

Author(s). (Year, Month Day). Title of article in sentence case. *Name of Magazine in Title Case, volume*, startpage–endpage. doi:10.restofprefix/nameofjournal.restofsuffix

Dehaene, S., Pegado, F., Braga, L. W., Ventura, P., Nunes Filo, G., Jobert, A., . . . Cohen, L. (2010, December 3). How learning to read changes the cortical networks for vision and language. *Science, 330*, 1359–1364. doi:10.1126/science.1194140

15. Article from an Online Periodical (Trade Journal) without a DOI

Author(s). (Year, Month Day). Title of article in sentence case. *Name of Magazine in Title Case, volume*, startpage–endpage. Retrieved from http:// . . .

Dehaene, S., Pegado, F., Braga, L. W., Ventura, P., Nunes Filo, G., Jobert, A., . . . Cohen, L. (2010, December 3). How learning to read changes the cortical networks for vision and language. *Science, 330*(6009), 1359–1364. Retrieved from http://www.sciencemag.org /content/330/6009/1359.full.pdf?sid=10c2a445-24c4-49ee-921a-2c5b04581efe

16.   Article from an Online Database

APA does not require the inclusion of database information. You should check to see whether your instructor requires it.

17.   Blog

Author. (Year, Month Day). Title of blog entry. [Web log]. Retrieved from http:// . . .

Levine, I. (2009, March 4). Thinking of texting a co-worker after hours? Does sex matter? [Web log]. Retrieved from http://blogs.sciencemag.org/scienceca-reers/2011/03/thinking-of-tex.html

18.   Book review (DOI)

Author(s). (Year, Month Day). Title of review in sentence case [Review of the book *Name of book*]. *Name of Publication, volume*(issue). page. doi.10. . . .

Preece, J. (2009, April 17). Growing up connected [Review of the book *Born Digital*]. *Science, 324*(5925), 338, doi:10.1126/science.1171818

19.   Podcast

Host/narrator/producer/director/writer. (Role of person/persons). (Year, Month Day). Episode. *Series.* Podcast retrieved from http:// . . .

Montagne, R. & Neary, L. (Hosts). (2010, May 10). Working to stop teens texting behind the wheel. *Morning Edition* [Podcast]. Podcast retrieved from http://www.npr.org/templates /story/story.php?storyId=126486142

20.   Video Clip

Producer(s) or author(s). (Year, Month Day). *Title* [Video type]. Retrieved from http://. . .

News on 6. (2010, February 26). *Broken Arrow teen survives driving and texting wreck*
[Video file]. Retrieved from http://www.newson6.com/video?C=121535&clip-
Id=4578883&autostart=true&redirected=true

21.   Wiki

Title of entry not in quotation marks. (n.d.). In *Name of Collaborative Work*. Retrieved
<retrieval date>, from http:// . . .

Texting. (n.d.). In *Wikipedia*. Retrieved October 14, 2009, from http://en.wikipedia.org
/wiki/Texting

22.   Electronic Book

Author(s). (Year of publication). *Title* [E-reader version, if applicable]. Retrieved from
http:// . . .

Author(s). (Year of publication). *Title* [E-reader version, if applicable]. doi:xxxxx

Speed, H. (2004). *The practice and science of drawing*. Retrieved from http://www.
gutenberg.org/etext/14264

Forms for Other Commonly Used Sources

23.   Dictionary Definition

Author(s). (Year, Month Day). Entry Name [Def. Number]. In A.A. Editor (Ed.) & B.B.

Translator (Trans.), *Website Title.* Retrieved Month Date, Year, from URL.

Reflect [Def. 1b]. (1989). *The Oxford English Dictionary* (2nd ed.).

24.   Television or Radio Program

Writer, W. W. (Writer), & Director, D. D. (Director). (Year, Month Day of publication).

Title of episode [Television series episode]. In P. Producer (Producer), *Series title.*

City, state of origin: Studio or distributor.

Lindelof, D.(Writer), & Bender, J. (Director). (2005, September 21). Man of science, man

of faith [Television series episode]. In J.J. Abrams (Producer) *Lost.* Oahu: HI: ABC.

25.   Film

Producer, P. P. (Producer), & Director, D. D. (Director). (Date of publication). *Title of*

motion picture [Motion picture]. Country of origin: Studio or distributor.

Winkler, I. (Producer), & Scorsese, M. (Director). (1991). *Goodfellas* [Motion picture].

United States: Warner Bros.

26.   Lecture, Speech, Address, or Reading

Author(s). (Year, Month Day). *Title.* Personal Collection of (the lecturer's name), school

or organization they teach for, city, state.

Baldwin, D. (2008, October 17). *Living a second life: Virtual worlds in the composition*

classroom. Personal Collection of Michigan State University, East Lansing.

27.   Personal Interview

While personal interviews are cited in the text of an APA paper, they are not included on the References page.

PLEASE NOTE: Original surveys (that is, those that you create, not surveys you find in other sources) should also be not be included on the list of references.

Organizing with Headings

Although headings are not always required, APA-style papers often include headings in order to make the paper easier to read and scan. Headings break up the main text of the paper into sections. In an APA paper, the introduction section typically does not have a heading. However, subsequent sections of the paper may have heading.

Imagine that your paper has four main sections after the introduction. Each of those four main sections would begin with a Level 1 heading as shown below. Then, if you wanted to break one of those main sections into two smaller sub-sections, you would use Level 2 headings for each of those two sub-sections. Always consult your assignment sheet and/or your teacher to find out if headings are appropriate for the paper you are writing. If you decide to use headings, follow these formatting guidelines:

Level 1   **Centered and Bolded**

Level 2   **Unindented and Bold**

Level 3   **Indented and Bold**

Level 4   ***Indented, Bold, and Italicized***

Level 5   *Indented, Unbold, and Italicized*

PLEASE NOTE: Unless you are writing a very long document such as a book or dissertation, it is highly unlikely that you will need to use all of the heading levels illustrated above. In fact, many papers that include headings use only first-level headings.

An Introduction to the Chicago Manual of Style (CMS) System 6

In addition to MLA and APA, Chicago style (CMS) is another citation system that you may be asked to use. First-year composition instructors rarely use CMS, but in later courses, your instructors in some disciplines may require you to use this style. The main goals of Chicago style are similar to those for MLA and APA. All three systems offer writers a uniform way to cite sources and format their papers, and all end with a list of resources used in the paper.

The biggest difference between CMS the other two systems is that papers written in papers written in MLA or APA cite sources in the main text of the paper with internal parenthetical references while CMS papers cite sources in endnotes (at the end of the paper) or footnotes (at the bottom of each page). Footnotes are somewhat more common than endnotes, but always check with your instructor to be sure which form is required for your assignment. The sample paper provided in this chapter is formatted in footnote style, but you can find many examples of the endnote style by doing a quick Google search.

Citing Sources in CMS

Each time you cite a source, you must insert a superscript numbered note (for example, 1) in the text that refers to an endnote or footnote (depending on the requirements for that assignment) that corresponds to that same note number. Footnotes are listed at the bottom of each page, and endnotes come after the text of the paper but before the Bibliography page that lists every source used in the paper.

Although this note system may sound difficult to work with, Microsoft Word and other word processing software systems make the process quite easy. In MS Word, you can quickly insert footnotes or endnotes by going to the "References" tab and clicking on "Insert Endnote" or "Insert Footnote." A superscript note number will be inserted at that spot in your text, and a footnote at the bottom of the page or endnote at the end of the paper will be added. If you delete the superscript note in the text, the corresponding endnote or footnote will also disappear.

The first time you use a source, include a full citation in the note (author's full name, title of document, publication information, and page number(s)). Examples of these full note citations can be found in the list that begins below. After the first time you cite a source in the document, list only the author's last name, the title or shortened title of the work, and the page number (for example: 1. Smith, 135) in your notes. If the exact same source is used twice or more in a row, substitute the word "Ibid" (Latin for "in the same place") after the note number in place of the author's last name and title and then give the page number (for example: 2. Ibid, 139).

Model CMS Paper

For your convenience, a very brief model paper is included at the end of this chapter to illustrate the preparation of a CMS style paper. Please note that individual instructors may ask you to deviate from some of the specific formatting decisions made in this sample paper. Instructors are allowed to ask for their own formatting requirements for page numbering, title pages, line spacing, font choice, or other issues. Thus, it is crucial that you pay close attention to any assignment sheets, models, or other guidance you receive on these matters.

Citation Formats in CMS

The following list provides sixteen common examples of Note (N) and Bibliography (B) entries in CMS. The (N) citations below are for the first time a specific source appears in the notes. Remember to use Ibid instead of the author's name and the title for subsequent entries.

Formats for Citing Some Common Types of Print and Online Sources-

22. Book (Including a Brochure, Pamphlet, or Graphic Novel) with One Author

Footnote or Endnote (N):

Note number Author's first name and last name, *Title of Book* (Place of publication: Publisher, Year of publication), page number(s).

[1]David Eagleman, *Incognito: The Secret Lives of the Brain* (New York: Pantheon Books, 2011), 104.

Bibliography entry (B):

Author's last name, author's first name. *Title of Book*. Place of publication: Publisher, Year of publication.

Eagleman, David. *Incognito: The Secret Lives of the Brain*. New York: Pantheon Books, 2011.

23. Book with Two Authors

N:

Note number First author's first name and last name and Second author's first name and last name, *Title of Book* (Place of publication: Publisher, Year of publication), page number(s).

[2] Arthur W. Chickering and Nancy K. Schlossberg, *Getting the Most Out of College*, 2nd ed. (Upper Saddle River, NJ: Prentice Hall, 2002), 122.

B:

First author's last name, first name, and Second author's first name and last name. *Title of Book*. Place of publication: Publisher, Year of publication.

Chickering, Arthur W. and Nancy K. Schlossberg. *Getting the Most Out of College*, 2nd ed. Upper Saddle River, NJ: Prentice Hall, 2002.

24. Book with Three Authors

N:

Note number First author's first name and last name, Second author's first name and last name, and Third author's first name and last name, *Title of Book* (Place of publication: Publisher, Year of publication), page number(s).

3 Gerald Graff, Cathy Birkenstein, and Russel Durst, *They Say/I Say: The Moves That Matter in Academic Writing, With Readings* (New York: Norton and Company, 2012), 39.

B:

First author's last name, first name, Second author's first name and last name, and Third author's first name and last name. *Title of Book.* Place of Publication: Publisher, Year of publication.

Graff, Gerald, Cathy Birkenstein, and Russel Durst. *They Say/I Say: The Moves That Matter in Academic Writing, With Readings.* New York: Norton and Company, 2012.

25. Book with Four or More Authors

N:

Note number First author's first and last name et al., *Title of Book* (Place of Publication: Publisher, Year of publication), page number(s).

4 Andrea Lunsford et al., *Everyone's an Author, With Readings* (New York: Norton and Co., 2013), 214-215.

B:

First author's first and last name, Second and subsequent authors' last and first names. *Title of Book.* Place of publication: Publisher, Year of publication.

Lunsford, Andrea, Michael Brody, Lisa Ede, Beverly J. Moss, Carole Clark Papper, and Keith Walters. *Everyone's an Author, With Readings.* New York: Norton and Co., 2013.

26. Translated Book

N:

Note number Name(s) of author(s) with each author's name in first name last name order, *Title of Book*, trans. first and last name of translator (Place of publication: Publisher, Year of publication), page number(s).

[5]Tadaki Kawada, *History of the Modern Suspension Bridge*, trans. Richard Scott (New York: American Society of Engineers, 2010), 156-157.

B:

Name(s) of author(s) with first author's name last name, first name order and all subsequent authors' names in normal order. *Title of Book.* Translated by first and last name of translator. Place of publication: Publisher, Year of publication.

Kawada, Tadaki. *History of the Modern Suspension Bridge.* Translated by Richard Scott. Reston, Virgina: American Society of Engineers, 2010.

27. Chapter from a Book

N:

$^{\text{Note number}}$ Name(s) of author(s) with each author's name in first name last name order, "Title of Chapter," in *Title of Book* (Place of publication: Publisher, Year of publication), page numbers.

^{6} Mark Battersby, "Sampling Woes and Other Biases," in *Is That a Fact?* (Peterborough, Ontario, CA: Broadview Press, 2010), 39-53.

B:

Name(s) of author(s) with first author's name in last name, first name order and all subsequent authors' names in first name last name order. "Title of Chapter," in *Title of Book.* Place of publication: Publisher, Year of publication.

Battersby, Mark. "Sampling Woes and Other Biases," in *Is That a Fact?* Peterborough, Ontario, CA: Broadview Press, 2010.

28. Anthology or Collection

N:

$^{\text{Note number}}$ Name(s) of editor(s) with each editor's name in first name last name order, ed(s)., *Title of Anthology or Collection*, edition number (if any) (Place of publication: Publisher, Year of publication), page number(s).

^{7} George McMichael and James S. Leonard, eds. *Concise Anthology of American Literature*, 7th ed. (Boston: Longman, 2011), 169.

B:

Name(s) of editor(s), ed(s)., *Title of Anthology or Collection*, edition number (if any). Place of publication: Publisher, Year of publication.

George McMichael and James S. Leonard, eds. *Concise Anthology of American Literature*, 7ᵗʰ ed. Boston: Longman, 2011.

29. Work in an Anthology or Collection

N:

Note number Name(s) of author(s) with each author's name in first name last name order, "Title of Work," in *Title of Anthology*, edition number (if any), name(s) of editor(s) (Place of publication: Publisher, Year of publication), page number(s).

⁸Ambrose Bierce, "An Occurrence at Owl Creek Bridge," in *Concise Anthology of American Literature*, 7ᵗʰ ed., Gorge McMichael and James S. Leonard, eds. (Boston: Longman, 2011), 1462.

B:

Name(s) of author(s) with first author's name in last name, first name order and all subsequent authors' names in first name last name order. "Title of Work," in *Title of Anthology*, edition number (if any), name(s) of editor(s). Place of publication: Publisher, Year of publication, page number(s).

Bierce, Ambrose, "An Occurrence at Owl Creek Bridge," in *Concise Anthology of American Literature*, 7ᵗʰ ed., Gorge McMichael and James S. Leonard, eds. Boston: Longman, 2011, 1461-1467.

30. Article in a Scholarly Journal

N:

Note number Name(s) of author(s) with each author's name in first name last name order, "Title of Article," *Title of Journal* Volume number, Issue number (Year): Page number.

9 Robert Clark, "A Tale of Two Bridges: Dangerous and Still Standing," *Leadership and Management in Engineering* 4, no. 3 (2008): 188.

B:

Name(s) of author(s) with first author's name in last name, first name order and all subsequent authors' names in first name last name order. "Title of Article." *Title of Journal* Volume number, Issue number (Year): Page numbers.

Clark, Robert. "A Tale of Two Bridges: Dangerous and Still Standing." *Leadership and Management in Engineering* 4, no. 3 (2008): 186-194.

31. Article in a Scholarly Journal Accessed Online

Journal articles accessed online are cited in the notes the say way printed articles are. In the Bibliography, they are cited the same way as printed articles with one addition: online articles need to include either a DOI or URL, depending on which one you have. If you have both, use the DOI number.

N:

Note number Name(s) of author(s) with each author's name in first name last name order, "Title of Article," *Title of Journal* Volume number, Issue number (Year): Page number.

[10] Naiju, C.D., M. Adithan, and P. Radhakrishnan, "Reliability Studies of Tensile Strength for Parts Produced by Direct Metal Laser Sintering Using Weibull Analysis," *Australian Journal of Multidisciplinary Engineering* 9, no. 2 (2013): 135.

B:

Name(s) of author(s) with first author's name in last name, first name order and all subsequent authors' names in first name last name order. "Title of Article." *Title of Journal* Volume number, Issue number (Year): Page numbers. http address or DOI number.

Naiju, C.D., M. Adithan, and P. Radhakrishnan. "Reliability Studies of Tensile Strength for Parts Produced by Direct Metal Laser Sintering Using Weibull Analysis." *Australian Journal of Multidisciplinary Engineering* 9, no. 2 (2013): 133-138. DOI: 10.7158/N13-GC02.2013.9.2.

32. Article in a Newspaper

N:

[Note number] Name(s) of author(s) with each author's name in first name last name order, "Title of Article," *Title of Newspaper* (Location of newspaper if not clear from newspaper title), Date.

[11] Jay Maeder, "In the Naming of a Bridge, a Lesson in Democracy Foiled," *New York Times,* Feb. 18, 2011.

B:

Name(s) of author(s) with first author's name in last name, first name order and all subsequent authors' names in first name last name order. "Title of Article," *Title of Newspaper,* Date.

Maeder, Jay. "In the Naming of a Bridge, a Lesson in Democracy Foiled." *New York Times*, Feb. 18, 2011.

33. Article in a Magazine

N:

Note number Name(s) of author(s) with each author's name in first name last name order, "Title of Article," *Title of Magazine,* Date, Page number.

[12] George Bukota, "Big Bridges; Local Spans Expanding and Receiving Facelifts," *Northwest Construction,* May 2004, 25.

B:

Name(s) of author(s) with first author's name in last name, first name order and all subsequent authors' names in first name last name order. "Title of Article." *Title of Magazine*, Date, Page numbers.

Bukota, George. "Big Bridges; Local Spans Expanding and Receiving Facelifts." *Northwest Construction,* May 2004, 25-30.

34. Article or Single Page from a Web Site with Known Author(s)

N:

Note number Name(s) of author(s) , "Title of Web Page or Article," *Publishing Organization or Name of Website,* publication/modification date (if given) or access date, URL.

13 Josh Levs, "Storms Slam Tornado-Ravaged Area as Town Tries to Rebuild," *CNN.com*, last modified May 23, 2013, http://www.cnn.com/2013/05/23/us/oklahoma-tornado-main/index.html?hpt=us_c2

B:

Name(s) of author(s). "Title of Web Page or article." *Publishing Organization or Name of Website*. Publication/modification date (if given) or access date, URL.

Josh Levs. "Storms Slam Tornado-Ravaged Area as Town Tries to Rebuild," *CNN.com* Last modified May 23, 2013. http://www.cnn.com/2013/05/23/us/oklahoma-tornado-main/index.html?hpt=us_c2

35. Article or Single Page from a Web Site with Unknown Author

N:

Note number "Title of Web Page or Article," *Publishing Organization or Name of Website,* publication/modification date (if given) or access date, URL.

14 "Building Big: Bridge Basics," *PBS.org*, accessed February 2, 2012, www.pbs.org /wgbh/ buildingbig/bridge/basics.html.

B:

"Title of Web Page or Article," *Publishing Organization or Name of Website* Publication/ modification date (if given) or access date, URL.

"Building Big: Bridge Basics." *PBS.org* Accessed February 2, 2012. www.pbs.org/wgbh / buildingbig/bridge/basics.html.

36. Book Review Published in a Magazine, Journal, or Newspaper

N:

Note number Name(s) of reviewer(s) if signed, "Title of Review, if any," review of *Title of Book*, by name(s) of author(s), *Name of Periodical the Review Appeared In* Volume number of periodical, if any (Date review was published), page number(s) of the review.

[15] Matt Hollrah and Frank Farmer, "Templates, Moves, Rules of Thumb," review of *They Say/I Say: The Moves that Matter in Academic Writing*, by Gerald Graff and Cathy Birkenstein, *Minnesota Review* 69 (September 1, 2007), 199-205.

B:

Name(s) of reviewer(s) if signed. "Title of Review, if any," review of *Title of Book*, by name(s) of author(s). *Name of Periodical the Review Appeared In.* Volume number of periodical, if any (Date review was published), page number(s) of review.

Hollrah, Matt and Frank Farmer. "Templates, Moves, Rules of Thumb," review of *They Say/I Say: The Moves that Matter in Academic Writing*, by Gerald Graff and Cathy Birkenstein. *Minnesota Review* 69 (September 1, 2007), 199-205.

SAMPLE CMS PAPER

Pleading for Rationality:

A Comparison of Two Recent Books

Edward Scott

IDS 398

Professor Pleasant

9 June 2015

Two recent books on human irrationality start with the assumption that logical behavior and decision making should not be considered the norm or baseline for our species. Both books describe human thought processes as a nearly constant war between our rational sides and our irrational sides. Daniel Gardner's *The Science of Fear* and *Sway: The Irresistible Pull of Irrational Behavior*, by Ori and Rom Brafman attempt not only to explain our irrational choices and behaviors but teach us to overcome our tendency to ignore logic in favor of emotion and fear when we make decisions. Although both of these excellent books look for the reasons behind bad choices, Gardner's explanations are much more satisfying because they are based on an underlying theory of irrationality while *Sway* opts for a more anecdotal approach that examines irrational choices one by one and thus fails to offer a unifying explanation for human irrationality.

In the "Of Two Minds" chapter, Gardner offers a familiar but nonetheless important model of the human mind that categorizes any human thought as originating from one of two systems of thought. The first system, which he calls, straightforwardly enough, "system one," is "the more ancient" of the two systems, the system that he calls "Gut"— our "intuitive, quick, and emotional" responses to various stimuli.[1] The gut reaction to snakes, for example, would be to avoid all of them because some have proven to be dangerous in the past. Gardner argues that "system two"—the "calculating, slow, and rational" system that he refers to as "Head"—is a much later development in human evolution and that "we have, in effect two minds working semi-independently of each other."[2] Later in the chapter, he says that we should think of every individual as a "caveman who wants to

----

1. Daniel Gardner, *The Science of Fear: Why We Fear the Things We Shouldn't—And Put Ourselves in Greater Danger* (New York: Dutton, 2008), 26.

2. Ibid, 27.

drive and a bright-but-lazy teenager who knows he should keep his hands on the wheel but, well, that's kind of a hassle and he'd really rather listen to his iPod and stare out the window."[3] In other words, the rational parts of our minds are clearly smarter, but are not always as engaged as the irrational parts of our minds. The remaining ten chapters of the Gardner book provide varied examples of irrational behaviors and choices, all of which boil down to the inability of the "Head" to overrule the "Gut."

For readers who lack the patience to read a three hundred page book that hammers home different aspects of a simple, unifying thesis, the Brafmans' *Sway* may be a more enjoyable, but ultimately less rewarding reading experience. Instead of referring to the same explanatory model throughout the book, each chapter of *Sway* offers a new explanation for a different type of irrational behavior. The first chapter begins with the story a series of bad choices by the pilot of KLM Flight 4805. Several frustrating delays and the pilot's desire to maintain his excellent on-time record led to the pilot's seemingly inexplicable decision to take off before he had clearance from the tower. Over five hundred people died in the highly avoidable collision that resulted from the pilot's impatience.[4] The authors explain the pilot's poor decisions by referring to an accepted truth in economic theory, the human tendency to try to avoid escalating losses. According to the chapter, the desire to avoid losses rather than maximize gains leads to irrational choices for everyone from consumers buying eggs[5] at the

---

3. Ibid, 31.

4. Ori Brafman and Rom Brafman, *Sway: The Irresistible Pull of Irrational Behavior* (New York: Broadway Books, 2008), 15.

5. Ibid, 17-18.

Scott, p. 4

grocery store to cell phone customers[6] considering which phone service to sign up for to Wall Street investors.[7] In the next chapter, the fear of deviating from popular but clearly outdated ideas is blamed for everything from underperforming college football teams[8] to the escalation of the Vietnam war and the failure of President Johnson's "Great Society." [9] Each new chapter presents another plausible explanation for certain irrational behaviors, but there is very little in the way of interplay between these explanations or development of a central concept from chapter to chapter.

Unlike *Sway*, Gardner's book has the merit of attempting a cohesive explanation for irrational behavior, albeit an explanation that even Gardner admits is bound to fail to combat irrationality because "that the brain that is doing this careful thinking is itself subject to the foibles of psychology."[10] The science in the book appears to be sound, but some readers might get a little tired of the message after a few chapters. In an online review of the book, Eric Olson comments that Gardner "guides us through the detailed mechanics of multiple studies that all essentially prove the same point."[11] Indeed, for Gardner, all

---

6. Ibid, 19.

7. Ibid, 22-24.

8. Ibid, 28-30.

9. Ibid, 33-36.

10. Gardner, *The Science of Fear*, 295.

11. Eric Olson, "'The Science of Fear': A Review of Daniel Gardner's Book about the Fears That Shouldn't Consume Us," *Scienceline.org*, October 15, 2008, http://scienceline.org /2008/10/policy-olson-science-of-fear-book-review/

irrational choices have one thing in common: a part of the mind that is older and in some ways works better than our more recently developed reasoning skills is in control when we act irrationally. That explanation might be somewhat simplistic, but at least Gardner is not afraid of making one. Anyone refuting his arguments would know exactly what to argue against while a response to the Brafmans would have to be as scattered as *Sway* itself. Perhaps that is why a review in *Publisher's Weekly* refers to the book as "timely but thin" and comments that the book "doesn't delve deeply into the psychological demons that can devastate a person's life."[12] In short, *Sway* is the more immediately enjoyable, but ultimately less important book. Anyone looking for a thorough, if not entirely defensible, explanation for irrational behavior should pick up a copy *The Science of Fear* instead.

---

12. Review of *Sway: The Irresistible Pull of Irrational Behavior*, by Ori Brafman and Rom Brafman, *Publishers Weekly* 255 (7 April 2008), 56.

Bibliography

Brafman, Ori and Ram Brafman. *Sway: The Irresistible Pull of Irrational Behavior.*
New York: Broadway Books, 2008.

Gardner, Daniel. *The Science of Fear: Why We Feart the Things We Shouldn't—and Put
Ourselves in Greater Danger*. New York: Dutton, 2008.

Olson, Eric. "*The Science of Fear*: A Review of Daniel Gardner's Book about the
Fearts that Shouldn't Consume Us." *Scienceline.org*. 15 October 2008. http://
scienceline.org/
2008/10/policy-olson-science-of-fear-book-review/

Review of *Sway: The Irresistible Pull of Irrational Behavior*, by Brafman, Ori and Ron
Brafman. *Publishers Weekly* 255 (7 April 2008): 56.

Sample Student Essays

We have collected several examples of student work created for assignments in First-Year Composition courses. In this chapter, you'll find the following essays:

- "The Language of My Feet" by Shelby Nicosia

- "Sex Appeal, Pain, and Heels: A Rhetorical Analysis of Melvin Konner" by Alexander E. Mosier

- "Shark Fin Soup, Anyone?" by Alexa Poirier

- "Two Truths and a Lie: An Analytical Examination of Rumor" by Mikayla Barnwell

- "Drilling the Coast: Prophesied Catastrophe or Forbidden Economic Treasure?" by Alessandro Parisi

- "The Truth Behind Vaccination" by Jami Pulley

Many of these essays have won awards in the First-Year Writing Contest, and they all demonstrate strength in several areas central to effective writing: organization, focus, development, coherence, style, and use and incorporation of authoritative outside sources.

You can use these model essays in two ways. One, your instructor may assign one or more of these works as a reading assignment, and you may discuss and critique them in class. Or, you may read one of these essays on your own in the process of thinking about your own writing. It's often useful to read student essays in a particular genre to help you get a feel for how you might write your own. For example, if your instructor assigns a narrative essay, you could read "The Language of My Feet" as a way of learning what an effective narrative looks like.

Though these essays have many strengths, they are not perfect. An important part of the writing process involves evaluation, of your own as well as others' writing. So, whether you read these essays in class or in your dorm, you should read them critically, considering which of their traits you would like to emulate and which you would treat differently. These are some questions you might ask yourself on a second or third read:

- Is the topic of the paper interesting?

- Is its main point (thesis) presented in a perceptive, clear and engaging manner?

- Are the main points of the paper organized in a logical and coherent way?

- Does the writer present information from authoritative sources effectively to support his/her point?

- Is the information from outside sources incorporated smoothly into the writer's argument?

- Does the writer use sentence structures and diction that bring clarity and precision to his/her points?

Considering these types of issues will help you determine the essays' strengths/weaknesses and heighten your awareness of the same issues in your own writing.

Nicosia 1

Shelby Nicosia

Prof. Rosner

English 101*78

15 September 2010

The Language of my Feet

It is anything but calm here. There are hearts throbbing, old friends laughing, rhythmic pounding of nervous feet trying to stay warm, and my head is racing. Racing, just like I am getting ready to do. It is my first marathon. A nonstop race of 26.2 miles, and yes, the .2 makes a difference. Marathons are not only down-right insane, they are also life changing. As I toe the line with the other thousands of people about to experience the same rush, I brace myself for one of the biggest and moving moments of my life.

Most people do marathons to test their limits, lose weight, and various other reasons. This is not my case. There is a deeper meaning in it for me. It is the annual St. Jude's Memphis Marathon in Memphis, Tennessee. The marathon is a big fundraiser to help support the children of St. Jude's Children's Hospital, a hospital for kids with life-threatening illnesses. This hospital is the epitome of "Heaven-on-earth" for these children. They take in kids even when the parents cannot afford the treatments, so fundraisers like these marathons are essential to keeping the hospital running.

Why is the hospital so important to me? When I was eight-years-old, my brother passed away from a brain tumor. He was a patient at St. Jude's for a few years before that. Ever since he passed away, I try to do what I can to help with cancer re-search and fundraisers.

I am not just running this race for self-satisfaction or to say, "Yes, I ran a mara-thon." I am running it for my brother and all of the other sick kids in need of hope.

The gun finally sounds and a stampede of runners from across the nation take off. Instantly, we are all in a world of our own. Many people do not see run-ning the way we do, but we view it as an art. It is our own language, one only true runners can comprehend. The world of running appears foreign to most others, but to us it is a way of life. We speak with our feet, not with our tongues. On this cool December day, however, we opened this foreign world of ours to the children of St. Jude's; because at this particular point in time, the running is not just about us. It is something much bigger. It is about the lives of these innocent kids.

With every step I take, we all take, our journey becomes words of hope and wisdom to their aching souls, and they comprehend it. Their appreciation radiates from their smiling faces. We pass by each kid bundled in warm, fuzzy blankets sur-rounded by their loving families. Shouts of "Good job, heroes!" fill my ears. These words give me a rush and a sense of joy because they are the real heroes, and it is such an inspiration to bring them hope through the simple strides of encouragement we create with the rhythm of our feet.

I near the finish line, exhausted beyond ever imaginable, and ready to give up. That is, until I look down at my shirt where it reads, "I am a hero." I think about the kids who never have a chance to be normal and carefree or create their own form of foreign language. I think about the kids who have spent their holidays in the hospital. Also, I think about my brother. He is the strongest person I have ever met, and if he can be strong, then so can I. I muster up the courage and strength from within, and I somehow push myself through the pain and across the finish line. I made it. I have spoken up for the kids who could not themselves with the rhythm of my feet. I have spread love and compassion through the simple language of my shoes. Most importantly, I have helped to make a difference in the lives of sick, innocent kids by using a language that seems more simple than English. I speak through running.

Mosier 1

Alexander E. Mosier

Dr. Arnold

English 101*23

6 December 2010

Sex Appeal, Pain, and Heels: A Rhetorical Analysis of Melvin Konner

In his essay "Kick Off Your Heels," Melvin Konner explains the sex appeal and physical illusions created by high heels as well as the health risks these shoes may cause. Konner describes society's attraction to small feet, lengthened calves, and certain curves that are emphasized when wearing heels. After his fairly optimistic explanation of why people are drawn to high heels, he abruptly implies that they are not worth it. According to Konner and other experts, the pain, injury and disfiguration that can come from high heels are not worth the sexual signals they produce. Konner uses the three basic appeals to get his point across to the reader: pathos, the appeal to emotions; ethos, the appeal to character and credibility; and logos, the appeal to logic. Even though he does some of these better than others, he still uses all three appeals adequately to express his views on high heels.

Using Repetition to Ignite Emotion

A common appeal that Konner makes use of is pathos, or the appeal to emotion. By appealing to emotions, an author can help sway the opinion of the reader. His most prominent practice of pathos found in "Kick Off Your Heels" is through the use of repetition. When discussing the damages that can, and often, occur from prolonged high heel wear, Konner lists many examples from abrasions to tendinitis (199).

In fact, he lists so many that it is difficult to not take notice. With so many possibilities laid out in black in white, the reader cannot help but feel remorse and sympathy for the victims of such pain and deformities. Konner also uses repetition, in a more optimistic way. He moves past his anti-heels argument to a pro-flats persuasion. "I think of adjectives that apply to women in flat shoes: lithe, graceful, earthy, athletic, sensible, fleet, dancing, practical, fresh, nimble, strong--and sexy, definitely sexy" (200). He uses so many positive adjectives to describe alternative footwear and leads the reader to feel hope and optimism in the fact that heels are not the only option for sexual signaling footwear. He's use of repetition continues to enforce the point he is trying to make.

Using Achievements and Sources to Create Authority

Konner works to capture the reader's attention through application of ethos. Ethos is the appeal to character and credibility, and by creating authority as an author, Konner becomes a reliable and trustworthy source. His credibility on high heel harm is implied both directly and indirectly. Konner's personal authority on the topic of human health is expressed in his head note. It explains that he is an M.D, a professor of anthropology, and an expert on health-care reform who has spoken to the U.S congress on the matter. Furthermore, Konner has three popular books on the subjects of human health (197).

Konner also speaks for his personal character by referring to other authoritative figures when appropriate. By using respected opinions on the issue of high heels and the harm they cause, he shows that he has done the necessary research to make his point as rich and factual as possible. Konner refers to an orthopedist, Sheldon Flaxman, who states that due to the damage that can occur from prolonged high heel usage, they should only be worn from time to time (199). The physical damage that is explained to come from high heels happens over extended periods of time. This means that heels are acceptable, and possibly even favorable in certain situations, but should be avoided for day-to-day usage.

Konner also makes use of less respectable sources that are still pertinent to the question. When discussing why people choose to wear high heels and the effects that they have on the opposite sex, Konner explains that men have learned to pick up on the sound of heels. "A convicted mugger has said, We would wait under a stairwell in the subway station and, when we heard the click of the wobbly spiked heel, we knew we had one'" (197-98). Though a criminal is not an academic or scholarly source, they are one of the most knowledgeable figures on this topic. Sometimes life experience makes someone more reliable than formal education. Konner makes use of that understanding.

Using Reason to Enforce and Support an Argument

Perhaps Konner's strongest argument comes in the form of logos, or the appeal to logic. The presentation of factual information creates inarguable support. Konner demands the reader's general logic to understand the harm of high heels. Konner lays out simple statistics and scientific evidence to support his central theme of high heel damage. He explains that podiatrists see far more women than men a year. This noticeable difference is mostly because of high heels and pointed toes (199). So many more women have problems in their feet because of the heels' force on the heel of the foot and the restriction of the pointed toe. Konner also explains some of the physical harms in depth. He states that bunions separate the big toe and the adjacent toe, allowing calcium to build up and eventually causing a permanent mutilation of the foot.

This type of medical problem occurs forty times more often in women than in men (199). By laying out indisputable statistics and scientific information, Konner makes it almost impossible to not agree with his position.

When explaining why women choose to wear heels he compares human knowledge of sexual signaling to animalistic instincts found in the wild (198). Though humans like to separate themselves from more savage beasts, we are still animals and know how to attract the opposite sex. This simple comparison helps the reader see what might cause a person to risk such deformity. Konner makes another simple, yet more comical, comparison by saying, "But for everyday wear they make as little sense as a three martini lunch" (200). Prolonged use of high heels is as logical as consuming a fair amount of alcohol at midday. A sensible person would agree that drinking like that does not make sense, so neither does continuous wear of heels. This small and funny comparison makes the reader think of the concept of heels on the same lines as alcohol consumption, a more common place concept.

The essay "Kick Off Your Heels" by Melvin Konner is a compelling literary work that demands the reader to see why people choose to wear high heels and the effects they can have on the body. Konner's use of ethos, logos and pathos assist the reader in understanding the reasoning behind high heeled shoes and the painful possibilities this footwear choice can cause. Some people will always choose to wear these shoes, but this essay helps inform the otherwise ignorant population on the topic of heels. Society as a whole generally fails to look deeper into the effects of what we want. At least there are people like Melvin Konner who can see the aftermath of common modern cultural rituals, and are able to express them to the masses.

Work Cited

Konner. Melvin. "Kick Off Your Heels." *80 Readings for Composition.* 2nd ed. Ed.

David Munger. New York: Pearson, 2006. 197-200. Print.

Alexa Poirier

Prof. Hensel

ENGL 101*87

10 December 2014

Shark Fin Soup, Anyone?

Caty Fairclough's article "Shark Finning: Sharks Turned Prey" outlines the overharvesting of sharks and their de-finning and how these processes lead to an unbalanced food web/chain, whereas Jimson Lee's article "Shark Fin Soup and Benefits of Shark Cartilage" summarizes why sharks should continue to be fished and used not only for food, but for medicinal purposes. Shark finning is the act of cutting off all of a shark's fins and then proceeding to throw the animal back in the water to perish. Shark overharvesting and also their de-finning is a major debate in certain parts of the world. There are some countries, such as China and Japan, which believe that they need to harvest more and more sharks in order to curb their hunger for Shark Fin Soup. These countries are their biggest enemies because they kill millions of shark species every year, without a second thought on what it does to our oceans and our world as a whole. There are other countries, such as the United States, which are trying to pass laws banning shark finning and shark fishing altogether. Oceana, a company that advocates for many marine animals, including sharks, has been able to end the selling, trading, and distributing of sharks and their fins in Illinois, California, Hawaii, Oregon, Washington, Delaware, and Maryland (Oceana). Both Fairclough and Lee make interesting points about the matter, but Fairclough is much more effective in her argument because she is able to make a connection with her audience by appealing to their emotions (pathos) and also by using imagery and writing techniques, such as cause and effect, process, and ethos to discuss real issues associated with shark fishing and finning. Lee examines how shark cartilage could be beneficial to certain people who suffer from arthritis, but he does not connect with his audience or use writing strategies, such as pathos, process, and imagery. He also does not prove to be a credible writer because he does not include sources in his discussion.

The primary issue with Lee's persuasiveness is that he does not credit his references. The article begins with his telling a story about him as a child and consuming Shark Fin Soup. "When I was a boy (and that was a long time ago) I remember eating Shark Fin Soup for New Year's Day dinner" ("Shark Fin Soup and Benefits of Shark Cartilage"), he says and from this, the reader gets a sense of authenticity because he is describing something he knows about firsthand. As the reader continues down the page, the article no longer is written by Jimson Lee; it is authored by a guest blogger named Darrell Miller. Lee writes, "There are several reports that Shark Cartilage is very beneficial to Support Proper Joint Function. Guest blogger Darrell Miller writes this article on the topic" ("Shark Fin Soup…"), so he has, essentially, copied and pasted another person's blog, about the topic, into his own article. He never mentions where the blog came from; he only mentions who wrote the piece. Since Lee does not properly cite his source, his credibility (ethos) is now questioned because he is not giving credit where it is due. Fairclough does the opposite in her piece; she has tags throughout the article leading the reader to further information on the subject. One example of her use of citation is when she discusses sharks that have been added to the endangered species list ("Shark Finning: Sharks Turned Prey"). She tags her source and this shows that she is acknowledging where her information has come from and this, in turn, adds to her integrity (ethos).

Fairclough's use of different writing techniques allows her audience to understand why sharks are a necessity to our oceans. Her use of imagery is visible as soon as the reader opens the article. At the very top of the piece, she placed a picture of a gloved hand holding a bloodied shark fin and a sharp knife splattered with blood ("Shark Finning…"). From this, the reader can immediately get a sense of what this article will target and it also appeals to their emotion. Fairclough utilizes pathos in order to elicit an affecting response from her audience before they even read the content. This is a good use of imagery on her part because if she had chosen another picture, it may not have had the same effect and choosing to have a graphic photograph as the main focal point of the page makes a statement about the issue. Lee, on the other hand, does not utilize any images in his entire article. He only includes Miller's blog and his small section of personal information at the beginning. Since he does not have any photographs, he is not able to elicit any emotional response from his audience about his case for using shark cartilage to aid in arthritis pain. This also leads to a lack of pathos because he is unable to make a connection with his readers.

Fairclough also utilizes two other important writing methods to aid her eloquence: cause and effect and process. Her use of cause and effect is evident when she describes the consequences of the decreasing shark populations. "When shark populations decrease, a ripple effect can spread throughout the rest of the ecosystem" ("Shark Finning…"), she states to describe how overharvesting sharks can lead to not only the depletion of one of the ocean's top predators, but also, it causes other populations of organisms to grow at an exponential rate. Her use of process is also prominent when she describes the procedure exercised to remove shark fins. Fairclough explains, "One way that humans hunt sharks is by using a practice called shark finning. This is the process of slicing off a shark's fin and discarding the rest of the still-living body, often by dumping it back into the ocean" ("Shark Finning..."). Her knowledge of this process shows her audience that she has done the adequate research to understand what takes place, and her citations reinforce this. Lee's article does not include these techniques, which causes his writing to suffer, on top of his not providing a proper citation. Since he does not incorporate any writing practices, he is unable to make a convincing argument because he has not employed any strategies to enhance his work.

Fairclough and Lee are on different sides of the shark fishing/finning issue, and their articles incorporate ideas that represent the points they want to make. Fairclough, being an advocate for sharks, moves her audience by discussing the distressing situation taking place in our oceans. Being a shark-lover myself, I would agree with her because I know how important these creatures are to our ocean's well-being. Lee does a poor job compelling his audience to take his side of using sharks for food and pain management. Fairclough is able to make individuals, even those who know nothing of sharks and their predicament, understand why we should be protecting these majestic creatures and making sure they are here to stay.

Works Cited

Fairclough, Caty. "Shark Finning: Sharks Turned Prey." *Ocean Portal: Find Your Blue.* Smithsonian National Museum of Natural History. n.d. Web. 2 December 2014.

Lee, Jimson. "Shark Fin Soup and Benefits of Shark Cartilage." *Speed Endurance.* Aryta Ltd. 19 June 2008. Web. 25 Oct 2014.

Oceana. Oceana. 2014. Web. 25 Oct 2014.

Mikayla Barnwell

Professor Sobota

English 102

29 March 2015

Two Truths and a Lie: An Analytical Examination of Rumor

Information that travels from place to place or even within small groups of people is often called a rumor. These informational tidbits are given a special name because of the quick manner in which they spread and for the fact that they are not always true. Debunking a rumor is not as easy as simply presenting the truth, especially in the political world. There are many different factors that affect the spread of rumor, and the attitudes of those involved play a large part. Using Gregory Rodriguez's theory of biased assimilation, one can further understand how prior knowledge and fear play an important role in political smearing, specifically surrounding Barack Obama and his religion.

Founder of the Arizona State University Center for Social Cohesion, Gregory Rodrigues wrote an op-ed for the *Los Angeles Times* called, "The Truth is in the Ear of the Beholder." In it he discusses his theory of how rumors are able to spread effectively and claims that they must contain information that the target group is likely to believe. Rodriguez calls this "biased assimilation." Based on the already known beliefs and wants of a specific group of people, an informational statement can be constructed that they are most likely to deem true. Rodriguez states that many try to use a lack of education to explain why large groups of people believe rumors that seem illogical and untrue to others; however, after a survey completed in 1994 on the conspiracy theory of Barack Obama's citizenship status, it was determined that education levels did not affect whether or not people believed the rumor. According to Rodriguez, people's insecurity about employment largely influences their choice to believe or dismiss a rumor (347). He supports his claim with Robert H. Knapp's theory that rumors are used to emotionally satisfy communities when groups of people are presented with unfamiliar news. Rumors tend to create the easy way out in complex situations.

In the article, Rodriguez notes that it is not always easy to dismiss a rumor even when the truth is presented. In some cases, the truth may make things worse. He cites an experiment done by Cass R. Sunstein that looked at how rumors are affected within political groups when the truth is uncovered. Sunstein presented a group of liberals and a group of conservatives with an article that stated Iraq had weapons of mass destruction, and the people were then asked to state their opinion on the subject. Next, they were given a false article that stated President George Bush's opinion on the issue and an article from the CIA stating that Bush's opinion on the subject was incorrect (Rodriquez 348). After reading the articles, the subjects were asked to present their opinions on the matter again. Sunstein's experiment showed that the liberals tended to disagree with the original statement, whereas the conservatives felt strongly that the original statement was true. Even though the conservatives were given information that disproved the original statement, it went against their political beliefs, so they opted not to believe it. Just because the correct information is given out does not mean that people will change their minds on any given subject. Rodriguez uses Sunstein's study to support his theory of biased assimilation in that if people believe strongly enough in something, they will only agree with or consider information that supports their previous beliefs even if is proven to be false.

Political elections are a prime example of how false rumors affect the beliefs of already strong minded people. Samuel G. Freedman's article, "In Untruths about Obama, Echoes of a Distant Time," explores the similarities and differences between the political campaigns of Al Smith in 1928 and Barack Obama in 2008. Freedman explains that in the midst of Smith's campaign, a photo was released depicting Smith at the opening of the Holland Tunnel. By the time the photo had circulated the whole country, there was a different story to go along with it. Many were told that Smith was going to turn the tunnel into a pathway to the Vatican so that the pope could give him secret orders. Freedman notes that before Smith, there had never been a Roman Catholic to gain a presidential nomination from one of the major political parties. He mentions that to some this may just seem as a misunderstanding that got altered in the passing of person to person; however, it was more than that. Serious anti-Catholic discrimination played a large role in the presidential election in 1928, according to Freedman's findings. Freedman ties the hate campaign against Smith to the accusations drawn against Obama during his presidential campaign in 2008.

During the 2008 presidential election between Barack Obama and John McCain, rumors surfaced surrounding Obama's religious background. Freedman notes how similar Obama's and Smith's situations are. He brings up the fact that in recent years there has been an anti-Muslim trend circling the US, and because of Obama's looks and Islamic middle name, many of his opposing followers claim that he is actually a Muslim. Freedman's article speaks about how people's fear of Muslims led them to believe that Obama would not make a good fit for president. Obama's situation reflects Smith's in that, in 1928, many people feared Catholics and believed that were dangerous. However, a large difference that Freedman makes apparent is that Obama is not actually Muslim. He states that in this day and age it is much easier for false rumors to progress even when the correct information is present. Although it was proven that Obama was really a Christian and was raised that way, his campaign managers were still forced to expend a lot of their time and energy putting the incorrect rumors to rest. Freedman claims that true facts did not stop people from believing that his rumored religion makes him a terrorist. In his article, Freedman draws an important parallel between Smith and Obama, saying that because of a particular religion, the two men were deemed un-American. He points out a valuable lesson demonstrated by Smith saying that the future of America cannot be successful "'if bigotry and intolerance and their sister vices are going to succeed'" (Freedman 371). Even though Smith was well before Obama's time, Freedman's article outlines the truth that rings in the 1928 presidential candidate's statement.

The spreading of false rumors surrounding Obama's religion as depicted in Freedman's article can be further explained by Rodriguez's theory of rumor, "biased assimilation." As previously stated, biased assimilation is when groups of people chose to accept or deny a rumor based on their already formed opinions or beliefs. The rumor that Obama is a Muslim is more believable to someone who actively dislikes him or did not want him to win the presidential election. They already have a strong negative opinion about him, and hearing this rumor only makes it stronger. In Rodriguez's article he states, "we tend to reject theories and rumors-and facts and truth- that challenge out worldview and embrace those that affirm it" (347). In this case, those that continued to spread the rumor surrounding Obama's religion felt as though it fit in with what they already knew about him. However, when it was presented that Obama was in fact a Christian and had grown up that way, they felt as though it challenged their views and they chose not to believe the fact. Rodriguez states "that the efforts at correcting rumors can sometimes even hurt the truth" (347). Even with the correct information out to the public, many people still chose to believe the rumor, which meant that those behind his campaign had to spend extra time trying to put the rumors to rest. For those who already believe the rumor, being presented with the truth may seem like a cover up and will make their belief even stronger. The truth doesn't always help if the public's opinion is strong enough to change it.

Rodriguez also makes a point to mention that people's fear about employment has a large influence on whether or not they believe a rumor. The rumor accusing Obama of being Muslim sent fear into many people because of their attitudes toward Muslims. After what happened on 9/11, many people directly associated Muslims with terrorists. In Freedman's article he quotes a Republican at a campaign rally for John McCain and Sarah Palin saying, "'Obama's a Muslim! He's a terrorist himself!'" (Freedman 370). Claiming that because Obama is a Muslim, he must be a terrorist implies that the person fears what would happen if Obama were to get into office. Having a rumored terrorist for a president creates panic within Obama's opposing community because of how he might change the job statuses in America. The community would not want to lose their job or have someone they feel is less qualified take it from them. The idea of having a Muslim at the head of their country and possibly within their own workplace is very unsettling for some people. They are aware of what that particular group of people have previously done to their country and are fearful of how it would affect their future if he were to be in control. Even though Obama is not actually a Muslim, the possibility that he might have been caused the truth to seem inconsequential.

Looking at factors that influence how a rumor spreads can shed light on certain situations and why people chose to pass a long certain pieces of information, especially in regards to politics. According to Rodriguez's theory of rumor, people chose to spread or stop rumors based on their already established beliefs and opinions. In the situation with Obama's religion, those that opposed him and already had negative feelings toward him, felt the need to spread the rumor that he was Muslim. Also, their fear of how he would impact their future lead them to further believe the rumor. Biased assimilation can be used to explain decisions made by groups of very opinionated people.

Works Cited

Freedman, Samuel G. "In Untruths About Obama, Echoes of a Distant Time." *Writing and Reading Across the Curriculum*. Ed. Laurence Behrens, Leonard J. Rosen. Upper Saddle River, NJ: Pearson, 2013. 369-371. Print.

Rodriguez, Gregory. "Truth is in the Ear of the Beholder." *Writing and Reading Across the Curriculum*. Ed. Laurence Behrens, Leonard J. Rosen. Upper Saddle River, NJ: Pearson, 2013. 346-348. Print.

Parisi 1

Alessandro Parisi

Prof. Hensel

ENGL 102*87

13 April 2015

Drilling the Coast: Prophesied Catastrophe or Forbidden Economic Treasure?

Nobody wants a rig in their own back yard. Towering metal behemoths rising from the ground have become images of filthy fossil fuels, environmental exploitation, and the industrial menace. Oil wells are the bane of many green advocates' vision of clean, super-modern utopias, but to certain minds they are another image: dollar signs. "There's just a win-win-win all around," Rep. Jeff Duncan (R-SC), says (quoted in Behre). Oil wells mean oil, which means energy, and in turn, money— for food, homes, and other jobs. Energy is a crucial part of the global economy, and so its value is apparent to anyone with good economic sense, but is a fleet of offshore drilling rigs really necessary for South Carolina? Despite recent conventions on energy development, significant shifts in oil pricing within the past several months leave more to be considered now than just "Drill, baby, drill!" These gains come with risks, and it is these environmental and financial risks that many local communities say are simply too high to justify any sort of drilling program off the coast. The vocal disapproval of coastal communities, combined with existing economic forces, indicate that now is not a good time to begin drilling; however, it is a good time to plan for when the forces of change will occur. Increases in fuel pricing and a stronger PR campaign based on safety and assurance from oil companies would provide South Carolina an opportunity to contribute to a broader story of energy independence and economic security.

Local opposition to offshore drilling has been spearheaded in many local news stories by Beaufort Mayor Billy Keyserling. His words stormed the local news in criticizing the idea of drilling off the coast: "'I think it is a huge threat without a whole lot of justification," Keyserling said. 'What is the impact to tourism of oil rigs? What is the impact on tourism of an accident?'" (quoted in Cary, "SC Policymakers Push for Offshore Drilling Despite Environmental, Tourism Concerns"). He is joined by nine coastal communities through municipal resolutions and several environmental groups such as Oceana and the S.C. Coastal Conservation League (Carnevale). Hamilton Davis, the Energy and Climate Director at the S.C. Coastal Conservation League, has summed up the many reasons for concern with offshore drilling for South Carolina. Unsightly oil rigs sprouting in the horizon would be an eyesore for beachfront resorts and properties (Davis). Additional contributions to fossil fuel use only serve to exacerbate effects of climate change, where states should focus on developing sustainable renewable sources (Davis and Oceana). There is the threat to local oceanic fauna with sonic seismic surveying techniques possibly throwing off natural feeding and migrating patterns or even harm marine organisms (Davis). Perhaps most prominently, there are the threats to local tourism, fishing, and wildlife from a major spill (Davis). Tourism alone is a $4.4 billion industry for South Carolina and supports nearly 79,000 jobs annually (Davis and Oceana). Myrtle Beach Mayor John Rhodes has said, "Tourism is our only industry, and therefore we have to be very protective [of our coast]" (quoted in Davis). Rhodes joins what has become a prominent consensus along much of the South Carolina coast in opposing offshore drilling. Just this March, Charleston became the ninth municipality to pass a resolution officially opposing an offshore drilling program (Carnevale). With the costs to local industries in the balance, local leaders are left with the question of what would happen if a spill were to occur and devastate the region much like the BP oil spill had for the Gulf of Mexico. They have argued that, given the meager estimates of Atlantic reserve studies from 30 years ago, a drilling program would not even be economically sensible (Welch). Hamilton Davis has described the impact of the total Atlantic reserve capacity as lasting for only 132 days for oil and 283 days for gas (Davis). So the offshore drilling possibility is not sitting well with many locals.

A clear dichotomy has emerged between local leaders and higher level government officials on this matter. Governor Nikki Haley has expressed support for offshore drilling, as have Senators Tim Scott and Lindsay Graham, who have authored bills in Washington for the opening of the Atlantic to oil drilling since 2012 (Byrd). There is certainly a higher pressure in upper level politics due to the pro-drilling stance of Republican Party members as well as a study released by the American Petroleum Institute claiming 77% of South Carolinians support opening the Atlantic to drilling (Cary, "SC Policymakers push for…"). An article by Ashley Byrd of SouthCarolina-RadioNetwork.com cites a study predicting over $87 million dollars a year in state revenue and over 7,000 industry related jobs by 2030 (Byrd). The American Petroleum Institute puts that number much higher at $3.7 billion in state revenue over 20 years ($185 million/year roughly) and a total of 11,000 possible jobs ("Offshore drilling not worth risks"). Yet another report by the Palmetto Policy Forum calculated the total economic benefit to the state at $15 billion and estimated any environmental costs to sum up to around $6.4 billion, including spill cleanup (Cary, "SC Offshore Drilling Report…"). Hamilton Davis points out the Palmetto Policy Forum's report did not take into consideration damages from coastal tourism losses (Cary, "SC Offshore Drilling Report…"). The report's conclusion is still, nevertheless, a wrench in the economic viability question. Graham's plan would designate the ten miles closest to shore as a buffer zone-- more than the official South Carolina range of three miles (Fretwell and Ocean (Offshore) Management). The next 40 miles after that would be up to the state government and any possible reserves located beyond 50 miles from shore would be open to Federal leasing (Fretwell). The Deepwater Horizon well was located over 50 miles from shore as well but in much deeper, and thus harder to reach, water depths (Behre). South Carolina would also receive 37.5% of the oil revenue in return (Byrd). Congressman Jeff Duncan SC-3 has been vocal in his support of drilling as well and has urged at least the consideration of seismic testing. "How do we know, because we are relying on 30-year-old technology?" Rep. Jeff Duncan (quoted in Cary, "SC Policymakers Push For...") says the most recent data of the possible Atlantic reserves, which were done in 1981 before the federal moratorium on Atlantic development, should be updated with modern technology so that we can fully understand the potential reserves lying off the coast (Cary, "SC Policymakers Push For..."). Considering the length of time and technological advances since, testing the possible drill sites with sound pulse sensors would be considered an early phase of any drilling activity in the Atlantic. It is also where concerns over the pulse sensors affect on marine wildlife come in, since they rely on sound waves that environmentalists warn could harm or interfere with whale or fish behavior, possibly with lethal consequences (Cary, "SC Policymakers Push For..."). However, Richie Miller, President of Spectrum Geo oil and gas survey firm out of Houston, has countered that argument, saying that federal rules regarding the safety of wildlife are upheld during survey and "protected species observers" are present on survey vessels to make sure they shut down scanning equipment in any protected regions (McCammon). The Bureau of Ocean Energy Development of the Department of Interior, which has endorsed the use of the technique (Cockerham), has released a study from similar surveys conducted in Alaska that found no harmful effect of the sensor equipment in the region they were studying ("Record of Decision").

Conversation about drilling in the Atlantic has been largely a non-issue since the 1980s moratorium, but recently it has grown as much in prominence as it has in resistance. In that time the United States experienced a growing oil trade deficit, importing 160% more oil in 2007 than it had in the early 1980s, amounting to roughly 60% of the nation's total oil consumption (EIA.gov). Lindsey Graham has been said to believe "oil and natural gas can help American energy independence," and indeed, since the U.S. began ratcheting up its own production that number has now fallen to around 40%, with private domestic land oil production growing rapidly since 2008, coupled with diminishing overall oil consumption nationwide (Cockerham and EIA.gov). This growing energy independence is coming just in time, as tensions in the Middle East and East Europe rise with growing aggression of big-oil players within the regions. Offshore drilling has been a whole separate matter. The Deepwater Horizon BP spill in 2010 essentially shut down new Gulf drilling with the Administration's following moratorium until a review of the BP safety systems were conducted: "'We're going to make sure that any leases going forward have those safeguards,'" President Obama assured the public (quoted in Johnston). Only recently has production begun to resume. In 2012, along with much of the talk of presidential year politics, and the release of Senator Graham's proposal, the idea of adding the Atlantic to America's growing energy portfolio began to spread. Fast forward to 2014 and the Administration's Department of Interior began studying the prospects of Atlantic drilling through its Bureau of Ocean Energy Management. January 27, 2015 they announced a press release detailing a regional strategy for offshore development, including South Carolina's Atlantic coast. The actual press release itself states:

> The potential lease sale would require a 50-mile coastal buffer to minimize
> multiple use conflicts, such as those from the department of defense and NASA
> activities, renewable energy activities, commercial and recreational fishing,

critical habitat needs for wildlife and other environmental concerns. ("Interior Department Announces Draft Strategy for Offshore Oil and Gas Leasing") This leaves plenty of room for fishing, tourism, recreation, wind turbines and whatever else coastal residents may desire. That is, unless, a large oil spill were to occur.

The environmental and tourism concerns largely boil down to a single scenario: a catastrophic oil spill similar to the infamous BP one in 2010. Sonic sensors, infrastructure changes, and economic feasibility are problems that can be or have been addressed through careful planning and market forces with minimal cost for what is potentially big gains for certain groups. The real inhibitive costs only come in if a spill erupts that costs billions of dollars in lost product, environmental damage, clean-up costs, and damage to tourism. That is when people would really be upset. Over time, actual oil spill frequencies have diminished per billion barrels produced (Anderson, Mayes, and LaBelle). The BP spill alone accounted for almost 91% of all the oil spilled on the outer continental shelf going back to 1964 (Anderson, Mayes, and LaBelle)! The next four largest spills occurred in the 1960s and the next three largest in the 1970s through 1980s (Anderson, Mayes, and LaBelle). Deepwater Horizon is much more a modern day anomaly than it is a norm, so it is hardly a realistic gauge of risk.

So if we are to keep that in mind, we then have to tackle the feasibility of a drilling program. No oil company is going to develop a reserve if there was not enough oil to pay off the huge capital costs, so assuming there is in fact a sizable source of energy off the coast, then that would mean an economic benefit for the state. Even if the numbers were to seem smaller compared to the $4.4 billion industry of Myrtle Beach tourism, for example, we have to realize that our economy is not made of just giant deals that surge $50 billion and tens of thousands of jobs overnight, but rather it is constructed of countless deals, many which are similar to the ones South

Carolina might consider through a drilling program, and together add up into the 2 to 3 to 4 percent GDP increases everyone looks forward to. Add to that the removal of the artificial overhead of astronomical energy prices and you have set yourself up for a fairly solid platform for growth. It is difficult to question the power of the energy industry and the experiences of states such as North Dakota and Texas, which speak strongly to the impact of energy on the economy. Cotulla, Texas is one such story: "Before the boom, jobs were few and poverty was high. Then, in 2008, oil company Petrohawk drilled the first discovery well, 2 miles deep into shale. It was successful and led to a drilling frenzy," (Block). Many of them asked similar questions to the ones residents of the Grand Strand are asking now, but they made it work, either through reasonable regulation or reasonable compromises.

Much of this was before oil prices began plummeting in late 2014. Like many things, time eventually brought the pendulum to swing the other way. The strengthening of the dollar was enough to bring down the price of oil by around $12 dollars a barrel itself, and together with natural gas, they have hit rock bottom prices with the surplus production throughout the country and worldwide economic uncertainty, or possibly, slowing demand (FRED). Conventional energy production is getting hit hard and so would warrant a re-evaluation of what we could expect to get out of an offshore drilling program with such risks as stated before.

A plan can be made to make the most out of South Carolina's offshore resources as possible without unnecessary risk. Oil companies won't want the oil off the Atlantic now with this market environment, but oil prices will rebound eventually, possibly up to $80 a barrel if production surplus levels out and exchange rates hold steady. If we were to adopt a plan similar to Senator Graham's proposal, then the state would retain much control over offshore development. Tack onto that plan the requirement for oil companies to contribute to a security fund that would be large enough to cover the bulk of the costs, perhaps about $20 billion or so, in the event of a major catastrophe. This could pay for much of the cleanup cost as well as account for much of any real damage to local economies. This would be held for the duration of the five year lease and be returned if no harm was done. Think of it like the security deposit on an apartment; the idea would be hold the oil company responsible in case they screwed up and let them be well aware of the value locals hold to their coastline. Is it a huge sum? Absolutely, but if the market gets to a point where demand continues to grow, supply stabilizes, and a company finds it worthwhile to invest their dollars in South Carolina (even with safeguards such as these in place), then there is no reason we should deny them our business. BP alone had over $284 billion in assets last year, so the money exists within the industry (Yahoo Finance). Also, the fund would be portioned out between individual companies depending on the size of their lease. If they are not confident enough in their safety protocols to put forth money in a fund that they would get back in time anyway, then South Carolina does not need their business. Maybe the state pays a little interest on that fund as further incentive for tying up so much of the company's capital, but if the gains still outweigh the costs, then where is the harm? There might even be a value for larger oil companies that can afford the temporary fund while their competitor's cannot. If oil companies agree to a responsible deal that is not designed to gouge them but simply to construct a protective mechanism for thriving, existing industries then the framework is in place for a reasonable compromise that plays to everyone's strengths.

The case against drilling in SC is compelling. However, it fits into a larger narrative that is very similar to others. Economic versus environmental concerns are often employed as political prodding tools and people can be drawn into an ideology of absolutes. We're fortunate right now to not feel the pressing need to expand drilling; however, in over a year's time the economic climate can change very rapidly. Drilling in the short term is hardly necessary and likely would present more risks to the local area than the benefits would really be; nevertheless, in time South Carolinians may find a day where demand through market forces would necessitate responsible drilling. Aside from any serious change in domestic energy procurement to alternative energy sources, this day will be present a serious choice for locals to consider, and it is one that should be prepared for ahead of time. Who knows? Perhaps the day will never come. Perhaps renewables will continue their advance and quickly grow to overtake fossil fuels. Let us not hold our breath just yet though. Human achievement is marked with many self-inflicted problems and for centuries we have been able to think our way out of situations. We can make these choices in stride. We do not need to force an immediate revolution through coercion and regulation when transition is more appropriate. Oil will likely be something of the past when something much more sustainable, cheaper, and likely cleaner comes along to take its place. The people and the marketplace will make that transition when it is ready. Until then, most of the world is still developing and they need something to power them into the technological age. Oil and natural gas will suit them just fine and it will come from Russia, or Iran, or America. Let us help them make America the practical choice.

Works Cited

Anderson, Cheryl McMahon, Melinda Mayes and Robert LaBelle. "Update of Occurrence Rates for Offshore Oil Spills." *www.boem.gov.* Bureau of Ocean Energy Management. June 2012. Web. 12 April 2015.

Behre, Robert. "Study says S.C. would benefit from offshore drilling." *www.postandcourier.com.* The Post and Courier. 17 September 2014. Web. 12 April 2015.

Block, Melissa. "Drilling Frenzy Fuels Sudden Growth in Small Texas Town." *www.npr.org.* NPR. 10 April 2014. Web. 13 April 2015.

"BP Balance Sheet." *Finance.yahoo.com.* Yahoo Finance. 10 April 2015. Web. 13 April 2015.

Byrd, Ashley. "Graham, Haley, Duncan push for SC offshore drilling." *www.southcarolinaradionetwork.com.* South Carolina Radio Network. 11 June 2012. Web. 12 April 2015.

Carnevale, Chris. "Charleston, SC Says No to Offshore Drilling and Seismic Testing." *blog.cleanenergy.org.* CleanEnergy.org. 25 March 2015. Web. 12 April 2015.

Cary, Nathaniel. "SC offshore drilling report: economy beats environment." *www.greenvilleonline.com.* Greenville Online. 18 September 2014. Web. 12 April 2015.

Cary, Nathaniel. "SC Policymakers push for offshore drilling despite environmental, tourism concerns." *www.islandpacket.com.* The Island Packet. 1 September 2014. Web. 12 April 2015.

Cockerham, Sean. "In South Carolina, leaders reconsider drilling along the coastline." *www.thestate.com.* The State. 22 April 2014. Web. 12 April 2015.

Davis, Hamilton. "Offshore drilling not worth risk to S.C." *www.statehousereport.com.* Statehouse Report. 30 January 2015. Web. 12 April 2015.

EIA.gov. U.S. Department of Energy, n.d. Web. 12 April 2015.

Parisi 11

"FRED Economic Data." *Research.stlouisfed.org*. Federal Reserve bank of St. Louis. Web. 13 April 2015.

Fretwell, Sammy. "Offshore drilling stirs waters in South Carolina." *www.thestate.com*. The State. 28 January 2015. Web. 12 April 2015.

Fretwell, Sammy. "Sen. Lindsey Graham's plan would open S.C. coast to offshore drilling." *www.mcclatchydc.com*. McClatchy DC. 12 June 2012. Web. 12 April 2015.

"Interior Department Announces Draft Strategy for Offshore Oil and Gas Leasing." *www.doi.gov*. US Dept. of Interior. 27 January 2015. Web. 12 April 2015.

Johnston, Nicholas. "Obama Says New oil Leases Must Have More Safeguards." *www.bloomberg.com*. BloombergBusiness. 1 May 2010. Web. 12 April 2015.

McCammon, Sarah. "Plans to Explore For Oil Offshore Worry East Coast Residents." *www.npr.org*. NPR. 12 March 2015. Web. 12 April 2015.

"Ocean (Offshore) Management." *www.scdhec.gov*. South Carolina Dept. of Health and Environmental Control. 2014. Web. 12 April 2015.

"Offshore drilling not worth risks." *www.postandcourier.com*. The Post and Courier. 3 September 2014. Web. 12 April 2015.

Park, K. "Offshore Drilling on Atlantic Continues to Divide East Coast and S.C. Residents." *palmettoscene.org*. Palmetto Scene. 12 March 2015. Web. 12 April 2015.

"Record of Decision." *www.boem.gov*. Bureau of Energy Management. July 2014. Web. 12 April 2015.

"Report to the South Carolina General Assembly The South Carolina Natural Gas Exploration Feasibility Study Committee." *www.scstatehouse.gov*. South Carolina Legislature.

"South Carolina's Offshore Energy." *oceana.gov*. Oceana. n.d. Web 12 April 2015

Sturgis, Sue. "Governor's Big Oil-Assisted Lobbying Pays Off in Obama's Atlantic
Drilling Plan." *www.commondreams.org.* CommonDreams. 31 January 2015.
Web. 12 April 2015.

Welch, Rodney. "Experts Disagree on Future for Oil Drilling Off S.C. Coast." *www.
free-times.com.* Free Times. 4 February 2015. Web. 12 April 2015.

Jami Pulley

Arnold

English 102

17 April 2015

The Truth Behind Vaccination

The autism spectrum disorder has been a source of concern for doctors and parents since it was first discovered. To this day, there is still a lot of mystery surrounding autism. Parents and doctors are still looking for causes and explanations to why autism happens. One of these proposed explanations is vaccines. A large number of children all over the world receive vaccinations. There may not be a better explanation for such a mysterious disorder than something that touches the lives of nearly everyone on earth. Given that vaccinations have caused adverse reactions in children, the rumor that arose in the 1990's that vaccination causes autism did not seem like such a stretch for people to believe. Soon some parents stopped vaccinating their children out of fear that vaccination will give their children autism. The controversy became so big that, around the entire world, people were talking about it. This gave way to massive studies and research. Through this research, scientists have come to an almost unanimous conclusion that, while some instances of vaccination being harmful are true, there is no link between vaccination and autism and the benefits still outweigh the risks of vaccination.

More and more children each year are being diagnosed with autism. Even though the number of children diagnosed with the condition is growing, the world's understanding of the disorder is still minimal (Glazer 649). What the world does know is that autism is a neurological disorder that affects a person's behavior in addition to social and communication skills ("What is Autism?"). The United States Centers for Disease Control and Prevention defines autism spectrum disorders as developmental disabilities that impair a person's ability to interact with others socially and communicate clearly. People with this disorder also display unusual behaviors and have strange interests. Many autistic people have different ways of learning, paying attention, and reacting to different sensations and emotions than people that do not have autism. Autistic people can also display learning and thinking abilities ranging from very gifted to extremely challenged. The display of the disability is usually seen in children under the age of three and lasts a person's whole life ("What is Autism?"). Autism is a serious issue that impacts more and more people each year, yet its cause is still unknown. People with autism suffer the symptoms their whole lives and in most cases are never fully independent. They often lack the skills to function regularly in society. As adults, the individuals need to be put in permanent adult care facilities or stay in communities dedicated to helping people with autism. With a serious lifelong disorder like autism, it is important to know its cause so that it can be prevented in future generations. Though it is still unknown what exactly causes autism, it is evident that it is a genetically based disorder and unrelated to vaccination.

There are many factors that make vaccination seem like a plausible cause for autism. Many agree that the controversy began because of the relation between the age that children receive vaccines and the age that parents start to notice the behaviors of autism in their children. This leads parents to make mental connections between vaccination and autism. Researchers, however, prove that autism is present in children before they are born ("Evidence Shows"). Another cause of misinformation on the vaccine controversy is the method of media coverage. Vaccination is one of the single most beneficial public health achievement of the 20th century. Another source states that, although this information is true, the amount of people that believe it is slowly plummeting because of "falsely balanced" reporting in the media (Dixon and Clarke

352). Falsely balanced reporting in the media is when reporters show the "controversy by presenting claims both for and against a link [between vaccination and autism] in a relatively 'balanced' fashion" (Dixon and Clarke 352). This means that, even though there is scientific evidence that vaccines are not related to autism, journalists present the controversy as if both sides are evenly balanced in evidence. This is unreliable because there is no scientific proof the vaccines cause autism and a lot of research that states that there is no link between the two (Dixon and Clarke 352). The first instance of misreporting came in 1998 when an article was published stating that eight autistic children had developed the symptoms of autism after they had received measles-mumps-rubella shots. This article was later retracted in 2010 and the research behind it reviewed to reveal that it was untrue. The author had changed the eight children's medical records to support his claims. By the time the article was retracted it was too late and people already believed the untruths of the article (Glazer 662-663). This all led to the worldwide vaccine scare in the 2000's.

Overall, most experts agree that vaccination does not cause autism. Such is the case with The Autism Science Foundation website, a nonprofit website dedicated to funding research for autism recognizes that, after an extensive number of studies, there is no connection between vaccination and autism ("What is Autism?"). Another source also supports this claim, stating that parents need to know that the American Medical Association, the American Academy of Pediatrics, the Centers for Disease Control and Prevention and any other medical professional in the world have reached the unanimous conclusion that there is no evidence to support the claim that vaccines cause autism (Koch 662). Over 1000 studies from 2004 and 2011 unanimously agree that there are no links between vaccination and autism ("Evidence Shows"). Through a lot of research and professional opinion, it is agreed across the scientific community that vaccination does not cause autism.

Even though vaccines do not cause autism they do have some serious adverse effects that should not be taken lightly. Some vaccines, such as the measles-mumps-rubella vaccine, have been known to induce seizures in children and even cause permanent brain damage ("Possible Side-effects"). Some of the blame for this is due to the lack of education of parents in regards to allergic reactions that children can have after receiving vaccines. Parents are not educated and, therefore, do not know the signs of sometimes fatal vaccine reactions. One woman, Michelle Helms, had her son Zachary die due to a reaction after receiving his immunizations. About the event she said, "Why aren't parents told about the real dangers these vaccines pose?... I could have seen the tell-tale signs of a vaccine reaction and done something to save his life" (Koch 645). There is even a government organization dedicated to reimbursing people who have had adverse reactions to vaccines called the National Vaccine Injury Compensation Program. The program has paid over a billion dollars to people who claim to have had an injury caused by vaccination (Koch 649). The effects of vaccinations are very serious and should not be overlooked.

Many worry that children today receive too many vaccines too quickly. They argue that the way the government forces children to get vaccinated in excess and in a very short period of time puts these children at risk of having serious reactions to vaccines. In past years children were vaccinated less, but today they are vaccinated more than ever before and at earlier ages. They often receive multiple vaccinations all in the same day and even when they are sick (Koch 649). Another source of problems with vaccination is lack of research of the adverse effects of vaccination. In regards to the lack of research, experts say that manufacturers do not take proper precautions when researching new vaccines. They say that vaccines are not researched enough and sometimes bypass essential steps before getting licensed. Some vaccines have gone directly from rodent tests directly into human clinical trials. This means that researchers skip testing on monkeys entirely and jump straight into tests on humans. Also, when there are issues in the monkey phase of testing, the signs that the vaccine failed are ignored and it goes into human trials despite the issues in monkeys (Koch 653). Manufacturers are more interested in the money they will make from a new vaccine rather than whether the vaccine is safe or not. Because of the lack of interest in safety from manufacturers, many vaccines had to be recalled after the recipients experienced injuries and even death (Koch 653). Some vaccines are still known to cause death in a small number of people ("Possible Side-effects"). All of the evidence presented gives adequate cause that vaccines should be researched more deeply and questioned on whether or not they are crucial to give to children.

Through all of the adverse effects, the benefits of vaccination still carry the most weight. Vaccines are one of the "safest pharmacological interventions for disease prevention available" (Koch 645). Health officials say that even if some vaccinations cause bad effects it is still safer to vaccinate than it is not to vaccinate. In regards to a recalled vaccine Paul Offit says, "A million children got the vaccine, and 100 got sick and one died. Yet now that it's off the market, if a million children don't get the vaccine, 16,000 will be hospitalized and 10 will die. It's still safer to get the vaccine" (Koch 645). Another educational web source also gives information promoting vaccines saying that, in countries with readily available vaccines, children today suffer from almost no serious diseases in comparison to the children of the same countries one hundred years ago. With immunization, serious diseases such as diphtheria, measles, mumps, rubella, pertussis, and poliomyelitis, which were often times deadly, are now prevented in children and are even eradicated from some countries entirely ("Practical Applications"). So the benefits of vaccination vastly outweigh the risks of vaccination.

Autism is a serious disorder that people live with throughout their entire lives. Although it is a serious condition it is still widely unknown what exactly causes it. What is known is that it is not caused by vaccination. Vaccination has no contribution to children developing autism. Autism is proved to be detected in babies before they are born. Autism is a genetically linked disorder and has no groundings in the use of vaccination. As for the vaccines, although they do not cause autism, there are still adverse effects. Vaccination has caused seizures and things as serious as permanent brain damage and death. Even having considered all of this, the world as a whole is still safer through vaccination. The number of deaths from vaccination is far fewer than the number of deaths there would be without vaccination. Therefore, even though vaccination is potentially harmful, it is still better for parents to vaccinate their kids than to not vaccinate them.

Works Cited

Dixon, Graham, and Christopher Clarke. "The Effect Of Falsely Balanced Reporting Of The Autism–Vaccine Controversy On Vaccine Safety Perceptions And Behavioral Intentions." *Health Education Research* 28.2 (2013): 352-359. *CINAHL Complete*. Web. 28 Mar. 2015.

"Evidence Shows Vaccines Unrelated to Autism." (Oct. 2014). Rpt. in *Vaccines*. Ed. Noël Merino. Farmington Hills, MI: Greenhaven Press, 2015. At Issue. *Opposing Viewpoints in Context*. Web. 25 Mar. 2015.

Glazer, Sarah. "Understanding Autism." *CQ Researcher* 1 Aug. 2014: 649-72. Web. 9 Apr. 2015.

Koch, Kathy. "Vaccine Controversies." *CQ Researcher* 25 Aug. 2000: 641-72. Web. 9 Apr. 2015.

"Possible Side-effects from Vaccines." Centers for Disease Control and Prevention. Centers for Disease Control and Prevention, 16 Apr. 2015. Web. 16 Apr. 2015.

"Practical Applications of Immunology." *E-z Microbiology*. Hauppauge: Barron's Educational Series, 2011. *Credo Reference*. Web. 9 Apr 2015.

"What Is Autism?" *Autism Science Foundation*. Autism Science Foundation, n.d. Web. 9 Apr. 2015.

Jami Pulley

Arnold

English 102

17 April 2015

Annotated Bibliography

Vaccination has been an issue of argument for many, many years. At first, the debate was that just vaccination is harmful, now it's branching into the fact that too many vaccines are harmful. There is a huge debate among medical professionals who argue about whether or not vaccination is harmful. Some believe that it is truly safe to give vaccines to children while some believe that there are serious health risks for children who receive vaccines. The question is: is there any truth behind the arguments that vaccines are harmful? Although the debate over whether or not vaccines are safe has been going for years and there are real people who still won't vaccinate their children out of fear, I will address whether or not the arguments against vaccination are valid. While some instances of vaccination being harmful are true, the benefits still outweigh the risks of vaccination.

The sources have different viewpoints on the argument but will reach a conclusion to the issue. The sources give both evidence from doctors and real people who were impacted by vaccines. Most of the sources use real evidence to back up their claims which makes them useful. The general consensus of the sources is that vaccination really is harmful but the risk of vaccination isn't more than the benefit. The percentage of children harmed by vaccination is far less than the number of children that would be harmed by the diseases that vaccination provides immunity against. Medical professionals who are against vaccines do not wish that they be done away with entirely, instead they want unnecessary vaccines to not be mandatory for children to

Pulley 2

receive. Given that the sources use information from both sides of the argument and find a

middle ground between the arguments, the sources seem to be credible and without fault.

Baker, Jeffrey P. "Mercury, Vaccines, And Autism: One Controversy, Three Histories."

American Journal Of Public Health 98.2 (2008): 244-253. *SPORTDiscus with Full Text*.

Web. 28 Mar. 2015.

The source outlines the history behind why people have a strong distrust for

vaccination. Thimerosal, an ingredient in vaccines, was found to contain mercury. This

created a controversy and distrust of physicians who had allowed the ingredient to be

introduced into vaccinations. The article give background on why this ingredient was

used in vaccines. The history of vaccination from their development to the present is also

outlined in the article. This gives historical background on vaccination as a whole and the

reason why there is a strong distrust of vaccines among parents.

The article is relatively current because it was written in 2008. It is not out of date

because the history of vaccination will never change. What happened at the beginning of

the history of vaccination will stay that way. The information is relevant because it deals

with the distrust of vaccines by parents. It gives background on why more and more

children are choosing not to vaccinate their children. The information in the article is

accurate because it has multiple cited sources throughout the article. I will use this article

to outline why parents distrust drug companies that create vaccines, making parents

scared to vaccinate their children against serious diseases.

Dixon, Graham, and Christopher Clarke. "The Effect Of Falsely Balanced Reporting Of The

Autism–Vaccine Controversy On Vaccine Safety Perceptions And Behavioral

Intentions." *Health Education Research* 28.2 (2013): 352-359. *CINAHL Complete*. Web. 28 Mar. 2015.

This article gives background on why the media portrays vaccines to be harmful to children's health even though that myth was proven to be untrue many years ago. The media portrays the controversy to be balanced when it isn't balanced at all. There is no real evidence that autism and vaccines are related. When the media paints it to make it seem like there is a debate, more and more parents get scared and don't vaccinate their children because they don't want them to become autistic. This way of portraying the controversy has adversely impacted the overall view of vaccines by the public.

The information was written in 2013, making it only a couple of years old. It qualifies as current and is not outdated. The article is relevant to the topic because it gives background as to why so many parents believe that vaccines cause autism. The news has made many parents scared to vaccinate their children because of the way they show the controversy to the public. The article is accurate because all of the information is cited and has multiple sources for the information in the article. I will use this article to present one of the reasons why parents are afraid to vaccinate their children.

"Evidence Shows Vaccines Unrelated to Autism." (Oct. 2014). Rpt. in *Vaccines*. Ed. Noël Merino. Farmington Hills, MI: Greenhaven Press, 2015. *At Issue. Opposing Viewpoints in Context*. Web. 25 Mar. 2015.

This source points out that there is no link between vaccination and autism. It states that the causes of autism are still unknown but the evidence that they have doesn't link the cause to vaccination. The article states that a large number of studies done in past years proves unanimously that there is no link between vaccines and autism. It also addresses the argument that too many vaccines can be bad for children. It says that a baby's immune system is more than equipped to deal with the number of vaccines that are given to infants.

The article was written in 2015, so it is based on current information with nothing outdated. The research that it cites are from as early as 2004, but the information provided by the research cannot expire and is still relevant to the topic. The article is relevant to the topic of my paper because it disproves that argument that vaccines cause autism, which will allow me to move forward in discussing the real risks of vaccination. The information in the article is properly cited. This means that the information is reliable and accurate and can be used as a source in my paper.

Glazer, Sarah. "Understanding Autism." *CQ Researcher* 1 Aug. 2014: 649-72. Web. 9 Apr. 2015.

This source talks about what autism is and the background behind the disorder. It gives the stories of real people that have had the disorder and their families. The purpose of the article is to educate people on what autism is and help people understand the struggles the people who suffer from it have. It also gives background on when people thought that vaccinations caused autism and states that the rumor is not true.

The source is under a year old so is still current. It is also relevant to my topic because it outlines the disabilities that come with having autism. It also states that vaccinations are not the cause of autism. It is accurate and has many citations to support its claims. I will use this in my paper to give background on autism and state that vaccination does not cause it.

Koch, Kathy. "Vaccine Controversies." *CQ Researcher* 25 Aug. 2000: 641-72. Web. 25 Mar.

2015.

This source outline the pros and cons of vaccination using opinions from qualified

doctors. It also has evidence from real people who have had their children be disabled

because of reactions to vaccines. The point of the article is to give the facts while having

the readers decide for themselves whether or not vaccination is worth the risk. The article

answers the pros and cons of vaccination, the likelihood that autism is related to

vaccination, and whether or not the doctors think that vaccination should be done away

with. It shares the accounts of a South Carolina woman who was forced by authorities to

vaccinate her second child after her first child had a bad reaction to a vaccine. They only

stopped pursuing her after she threatened to attack them and leave the state.

The source is over fourteen years old, but the portions of it that could expire over

time will not be used in my paper. I will instead focus on the accounts of people and

doctors as they pertain to vaccination today. The article is very relevant to my topic. It

directly addresses the question that the thesis of my paper proposes. It also provides other

information that will help in proving the point of my paper. The article is accurate overall

because of the accounts from doctors and the extensive list of citations used to write the

article.

"Possible Side-effects from Vaccines." *Centers for Disease Control and Prevention.* Centers for

Disease Control and Prevention, 16 Apr. 2015. Web. 16 Apr. 2015.

The purpose of this web source is to educate people on the possible effects of

vaccines. It lists all the major vaccinations that children receive and lists the side effects

from mild to severe and most common to very rare. It also acknowledges that there are

Pulley 6

side effects to vaccines and that they can be helped through close observation and

reporting to a doctor.

The source was updated the same day that I accessed it so it is being maintained

for accuracy regularly. It is accurate because it is being published through the CDC

website. It is relevant to my topic because it outlines the adverse effects that vaccines can

cause in children, some of them very serious. I will use this source in my paper to state

some of the more serious effects that vaccines can have in children.

"Practical Applications of Immunology." *E-z Microbiology.* Hauppauge: Barron's Educational

Series, 2011. Credo Reference. Web. 9 Apr 2015.

The purpose of this source is to educate medical students on the uses of

immunization. It gives background and evidence behind immunization and the benefits of

it. The source also gives information in an informative way that is easy to understand and

navigate.

It is relatively current because it was published in 2011, but that does not affect

the accuracy because the information in the source has not changed over time. It outlines

some of the benefits of vaccination and states why it is important that immunizations are

given to people. I will use it as background on some of the benefits of giving children

vaccines and why it is better to vaccinate children than not to vaccinate them.

"What Is Autism?" *Autism Science Foundation.* Autism Science Foundation, n.d. Web. 9 Apr.

2015.

This article is published by the Autism Science Foundation which is a foundation

dedicated to researching the causes and treatments for autism. The webpage I used is and informative passage that's goal is to educate people on what autism is. It gives the symptoms of autism and history behind the disorder.

There is no date in which the article was written but the information in the article is based purely on facts that cannot expire with time. It is accurate and gives citations for the information stated in the article. It is also relevant to my topic because it outlines the symptoms of autism. It also gives background on the relation between autism and the vaccine controversy. I will use the source to help the reader better understand autism.

Song, Geoboo. "Understanding Public Perceptions Of Benefits And Risks Of Childhood Vaccinations In The United States." *Risk Analysis: An International Journal* 34.3 (2014): 541-555. *SPORTDiscus with Full Text*. Web. 28 Mar. 2015.

The purpose of the article is to analyze what the general public thinks about vaccination. There has been a reemergence of preventable diseases because of parents' growing fear that their children will get autism or some other disease from vaccination. The article goes into the reason why parents choose not to vaccinate their children and the misconceptions they have about the balance of risks and benefits of vaccination.

The article was written in 2014, meaning that it is based on current information. The sources are all current so none of the information is outdated and is all still relevant to the topic. The article is relevant in that it explains why some parents choose not to immunize their children. It also lists the reasons why parents choose not to vaccinate and the arguments that those parents have against vaccination. The information in the article is known to be accurate because all of the information in the article is cited. I will use this source to get background on reasons why parents choose not to vaccinate their children.